£25·00

SOCIAL CLASS, STATUS AND TEACHER TRADE UNIONISM:
The Case of Public Sector Further and Higher Education

Many professionals working in the public sector, whether as doctors, teachers or nurses, feel that their interests and those of the institutions in which they work are under attack. This book examines some of the causes underlying the growing resentment of public sector professionals, focusing on the teachers in the polytechnics and colleges of further and higher education and on their union, once the *Association of Teachers in Technical Institutions*, now the *National Association of Teachers in Further and Higher Education*. It looks in depth at the relationship between professional commitment and trade union activism and at the limits employee status within a bureaucratic control structure can impose on professional self-management and control.

The book provides both an important social history of the teachers and teaching in this sector and an incisive analysis of the nature and development of 'professional trade unionism'.

Sandra Turner is Senior Lecturer in Sociology at the Ealing College of Higher Education.

Social Class, Status and Teacher Trade Unionism:

The Case of Public Sector
Further and Higher Education

SANDRA TURNER

CROOM HELM
London • New York • Sydney

© 1988 Sandra Turner
Croom Helm Ltd, Provident House, Burrell Row,
Beckenham, Kent, BR3 1AT

Croom Helm Australia, 44-50 Waterloo Road,
North Ryde, 2113, New South Wales

Published in the USA by
Croom Helm
in association with Methuen, Inc.
29 West 35th Street
New York, NY 10001

British Library Cataloguing in Publication Data

Turner, Sandra
    Social class, status and teacher trade
    unionism.
    1. National Association of Teachers in
    Further and Higher Education — History
    I. Title
    331.88′1137812′0942   LB2335.865.G7
    ISBN 0-7099-4359-8

Library of Congress Cataloging-in-Publication Data

ISBN 0-7099-4359-8

Printed and bound in Great Britain
by Billing & Sons Limited, Worcester.

Contents

Contents

To Jack Hendy

Foreword

It is a paradox of British society that it hides what it is best at. It hid its industrialism in the nineteenth century behind a screen of arcadian greenery and continues to do so in the twentieth-century period of high tech. It hid its inventive genius behind a facade of ancient continuity. It hid its capacity to educate industrial and technological experts behind grammar schools and ancient universities.

One consequence has been the invisibility of industrial and technical teachers who have lived under the shadow of dons, whether from Cambridge or Sussex, their persistent excellence obscured by a metropolitan culture which contrived to ignore the historical fact that Britain was the first industrial nation. That the splendid universities of the modern provincial cities in Birmingham, Manchester, Leeds or Sheffield owed a great deal to teachers of the industrial arts and sciences in such nineteenth-century colleges as Josiah Mason or Owen's has, at least until recently, gone unrecognised. The institutional path from 'night school' or technical college to technological university has been the path into social visibility.

Dr Turner's book is a welcome antidote to the conventional focus on the universities of histories of higher education. It tells the story of the men and women who have gone about the task of intellectual labour in the service of commerce, industry and administration on which the economic life of the nation (and indeed the export of industrial skill to other nations) has depended for the last century and a half. Moreover it is more than an antidote; it is an empirical study of permanent value to those who wish to understand the growth and fortune (including misfortune) of the teaching professions as a whole.

The story corrects many a false image. The history of university teachers tends to be written as either the slow extension of the way of work of the Oxford tutorial fellow or of the imitation of the German professorial hierarchy. Dr Turner's NATFHE is neither and is in any case an

Foreword

upthrust from the wider, more popular base of secondary school teaching. Thus she is able to remind us how technical teachers have been the agents for the promotion of mobility of many boys and some girls out of the classical urban working class, and it emerges that they themselves have often been socially promoted by the enlightenment they spread. In the same context the relation of college teaching to union organisation, which she relates so well, has a special significance. While ideologies compete in defining the class and professional position of further and higher education teachers, the facts as Dr Turner marshals them, serve to inform the debate.

It may well be that future historians will describe educational developments in the second half of the twentieth century in Britain as a failed thrust towards universal education beyond school despite and partly because of the programme of university expansion associated with the Robbins Report. We now have twice as many university teachers as we had students at the beginning of the century. But Robbins also ushered in a binary system the 'other side' of which is Dr Turner's concern. The Principal of Leeds Polytechnic, Christopher Price, has asserted that Britain has the worst provision of higher education of any country in the western world. It is in such a perspective that we must recognize the present discontents of a body of teachers to whom the nation owes a debt which ought to be repaid.

A. H. Halsey

Preface

This book is about teachers in public sector further and higher education and their union, once the <u>Association of Teachers in Technical Institutions</u> (the ATTI), now the <u>National Association of Teachers in Further and Higher Education</u> (NATFHE). These teachers work in the colleges of further and higher education and in the polytechnics in England and Wales and number over 90,000 in total. The colleges have their origins in the technical colleges and night schools of the late nineteenth century and owe much of their contemporary character and status to that fact. Nevertheless, from the 1960s onwards they diversified to such an extent that for many the once familiar 'tech' became a singular misnomer. What is now called non-advanced further education (NAFE) not only comprises work-related or directly vocational schemes, but also the sort of 'O' and 'A' level work taught in the schools. At the other end of the scale, the polytechnics and colleges of higher education engage primarily in advanced further education (AFE) at degree and postgraduate level. Whilst the original binary philosophy which signalled the development of such courses outside the university sector implied that they be vocationally relevant in keeping with the technical college tradition, that relevance was always broadly interpreted and by the seventies the social sciences had found a relatively happy home there, either as degrees in their own right or servicing the more directly vocational business studies courses which were mushrooming at that time.

During the seventies, this process of diversification was completed with the 'rationalisation' of teacher education. Many teacher training colleges were forced to close, others to merge with existing polytechnics or with other colleges to become what are now known as the colleges of higher education. These colleges soaked up much of the 'spare capacity' from the teacher training colleges, mainly in the form of humanities teaching. In January 1976, the ATTI merged with the smaller <u>Association of Teachers in Colleges and Departments of Education</u> and changed its name to NATFHE in a rather belated recognition of the post-war developments which had rendered the terms technical teacher and technical education somewhat obsolete. It has since merged with the <u>Association of Continuative Education</u> and also the <u>Association of Teachers in Penal Establishments</u> to become the only single union representing all teachers in public sector post-school education. It is the history of these teachers, their work and their organisation which is the object of this study.

As such this is a study in the history of education and of educational ideas as well as a study in the sociology of occupations. But in fact the research was originally conceived within the context of the debate about the nature and significance of white-collar trade unions. Teacher militancy always seems to take people by surprise, but it is not a new thing as this and other studies have shown. Neither were the school teachers exempt from the wave of white-collar militancy which characterised the late sixties and early seventies, militancy which gave rise to the question as to whether white-collar unions, including teacher unions, were any different from those of manual workers. Many believed that they were. Starting from the premise that white-collar workers were middle class in the Weberian sense, great emphasis was placed on their status-consciousness and individualism. Thus when white-collar workers did join trade unions, it was because they saw them as something to be used rather than as something in which to believe. Union membership for them, therefore, had little class significance. It was neither an index of objective proletarianisation nor of a change in consciousness, a position in direct contradistinction to those both inside and outside the trade union movement who had assumed that for all their warts, associations of white-collar workers were in practice beginning to take on the characteristics of those of traditional manual workers, thereby becoming the kind of class organisations those unions had always been taken to be.

The debate was further complicated by the professional status and aspirations of the teachers. Many early sociologists had assumed that professional status placed the individual above the normally antagonistic relations between capital and labour, a position which now seemed untenable as more and more came to be employed in large organisations and by the state. Indeed the special status of both the professionals and their associations had been debunked to such an extent by the early seventies that some academics prominent in the field felt confident enough to assert that rather than being distinct from trade unions, professional associations could more accurately be portrayed as the craft unions of a different social group - by implication denuding not only white-collar unions but all trade unions of any necessary class significance. More recently still, work within a neo-Marxist tradition has resurrected the class significance of white-collar and professional trade unionism but from a totally different point of view. For many of these writers not only do these strata constitute a different social group from manual workers, they constitute a different social class, the 'new middle-class', and in so far as their associations represent the interests of that class (for example, where teachers are concerned, as part of the ideological state apparatus) far from being the progressive embodiment of proletarian-isation, they can be bourgeois and reactionary - the class enemy within, if you like.

But whatever the theoretical predilections of writers in the field, all have agreed that whilst much has been said, too little is known in the sense that empirical work, especially of a historical nature, is too thin on the ground to resolve such important questions. This study of the ATTI from its inception as a self-proclaimed professional association in 1904 to its development into a self-conscious trade union is a modest attempt to help redress that balance. Research for the study has taken place over a period of 15 years, from 1972 to the present. The history of the Association was written from its own archives, in particular from its official journal, Executive and Council Minutes. Where possible, reference was also made to the educational press. In addition, during the period 1973 to 1976 prominent members of the Association both past and present were interviewed as key informants. This included all three General Secretaries from 1954 to that date together with long-serving Council and Executive members. Care was taken to include informants of all political persuasions to control for selectivity in the interpretation of past events. Interviews of both branch activists and members were carried out in the Manchester and Bristol areas and a postal questionnaire was sent to 1000 members of the West Midlands Division, then the largest division in the country. In this way it was hoped to cast the net as widely as possible at the same time as allowing the history of the union to be written by those most intimately concerned.

Whilst empirical in thrust, the research was, of course, guided by the writer's own values and theoretical preferences. I could accept neither the rather blithe denial of any significant class difference between the traditional professional associations on the one hand, and trade unions on the other nor the neo-Marxist attempts to keep the working class pure. I preferred a good old-fashioned Marxist wage-labour definition of class, supplemented of course by the appropriate contextual variables. It was armed with this preference that I set out to examine the nature of professionalism and trade unionism amongst an increasingly significant group of teachers, the technical teachers as they once were, the college lecturers as they are now and of which the writer is one. The history of NATFHE's first ten years, therefore, has been written with the aid of a significant amount of participant observation. However, special thanks is due to all those ATTI and NATFHE members, branch secretaries and officers who gave freely of their time and without whom the research would not have been possible. It is they who are in practice resolving any contradiction there might be between real professionalism and trade unionism in action to defend their sector of education in what threatens to become an increasingly hostile climate.

PART ONE

THE GROWTH OF A PROFESSION

Modest Beginnings

ENLIGHTENED SELF-INTEREST

It is to developments in the provision of education in the second half of the last century that we owe the creation of a body of men dependent for their livelihood and status on technical teaching as such. The Great Exhibition of 1851 had caused some concern amongst the ranks of educationalists, industrialists and politicians alike that Britain was in danger of losing her industrial pre-eminence if she did not begin to pay more attention to scientific and technical education. The resulting agitation led to the setting up of the Department of Science and Art in 1853 and the establishment of examinations by that body in 1859 to encourage the education of artisans in the scientific principles underlying their trades. The system of examination was one of payment-by-results, limited to the results of students from 'the industrial classes'. Secondary and elementary school teachers became qualified to teach these subjects and set up evening classes to earn money to supplement their incomes. With this incentive, the Department of Science and Art examinations flourished. The numbers increased from about 1,300 in 1861 to 34,000 in 1870 and passed the 100,000 mark in 1887.[1] During the early years of these examinations, scientific and technical teaching was scarcely ever followed as a profession, but only as an addition to more profitable or secure employment elsewhere. In 1871 for example, two-thirds of the teachers employed by the Science and Art Department under this payment-by-results system were full-time elementary teachers. Not more than eight teachers in the whole country earned their living by science teaching alone.[2]

Nevertheless, it is to the institution of these examinations that we owe the first generation of technical teachers. According to C.T. Millis, Principal of The Borough Polytechnic from 1892 to 1922:

The classes were attended by large numbers of the more skilled workmen engaged chiefly in the

Engineering and Building Trades, who, intelligent and anxious for self-improvement, saw in them the opportunity of gaining knowledge of Science and Art which would assist them to understand some of the problems connected with their trade, make them better workmen and qualify some of them for higher positions ... Many of the students of these classes have made their mark in trade and industries. Some of the best students who had practical acquaintance with either the Engineering, Building or other trades, became excellent teachers when the Technical Education Movement became general from 1880 onwards.[3]

The Technical Education Movement referred to by Millis gathered impetus after the 1867 International Exhibition in Paris which revealed 'a state of affairs highly discreditable to this country'. Its avowed aims were 'to provide theoretical and practical instruction for artisans and others engaged in industry; an adequate supply of teachers of technology with proper schools in industrial areas and thirdly, proper scholarships with openings as teachers or as original researchers in applied science'.[4]

The efforts of private and corporate philanthropy combined with increasing state aid saw the near achievement of these aims by the end of the century. For example, 1872 witnessed a movement away from the idea of technical education as a smattering of science for the working man with the setting up of higher level technological examinations by the Society of Arts, although these examinations (open to those already qualified in the more elementary Department of Science and Art examinations) were slow to get off the ground. Since no payments were offered to teach them, no instruction was provided and all candidates were completely self-taught. This situation was remedied, however, in 1880 with the establishment of the City and Guilds of London Institute for the Advancement of Technical Education. Its first act was to take over the technological examinations of the Royal Society and give financial assistance to instruction, again through a system of payment-by-results. In so doing, the number of candidates offering themselves for examination rose from 68 in 1877 to 2,397 in 1883 and by 1888 there were 6,166.[5]

It was not intended that the City and Guilds should be merely an examining body, however. During the 1870s the

Livery Companies had planned to create a 'City and Guilds Industrial University' and the Institute itself was founded specifically as a teaching institute. In 1881, it opened the Finsbury Technical College to provide both day and evening classes in such vocational subjects as engineering and building and in the principles of mathematics, mechanical drawing and science upon which such trades depended. Dent, for example, tells us that the Technical College aimed to be 'a model trade school for the instruction of artisan and other persons preparing for intermediate posts in industrial work'.[6] Whilst the first such technical college in England, before long many other institutes were established along similar lines.

A movement parallel to these developments in the provision of science and technical instruction was that of the London polytechnics. The first of the polytechnics, Regent Street, was opened in 1881 thanks to the efforts of the philanthropist, Quintin Hogg. Within sixteen years there were nine of them in London with an enrolment of 26,000 students, a large number of whom were manual workers. This large proportion of manual workers studying at the London polytechnics was due, it seems, to their willingness to offer more specifically trade instruction than the Department of Science and Art examinations had hitherto allowed. For example, Millis tells us that in 1892-3 the smallness of the Borough Polytechnic's grant from the Science and Art Department had been questioned. 'This was due,' he explained, 'to the attitude of the Governing Body who had left the Principal free to choose the subjects of instruction best suited to the requirements of workers in a number of trades for which being of a technological character, no grant could then be obtained from the Department.'[7] Quintin Hogg kept his early trade classes going out of his own, not inconsiderable, pocket. But what gave strength and permanency to the movement were the funds appropriated under the City Parochial Charities Act of 1883 which was made possible by the popular definition of the work done in the polytechnics as 'rescue work' for the poor. Further funds were made available to the London polytechnics, as indeed to technical instruction generally, after 1892 with Goschen's Local Taxation Act. This Act placed the sum of £750,000 at the disposal of the local authorities specifically for technical education. The money, popularly known as 'whiskey money', was originally intended to compensate publicans who had lost their licence!

Finally, the Technical Instruction Act was passed in 1889. This Act empowered county and borough councils to levy rates to establish technical institutes for 'teaching the principles of science and art applicable to industries' and 'the application of special branches of science and art to specific industries and employments'. Such was the effect of this Act that at the turn of the century a chief inspector of technical instruction could report to the Board of Education:

> Nothing in English education is more remarkable than the manner in which special institutes for the purposes of science, art and technical work have sprung up all over the country during the last twenty years. When I began as an inspector there were scarcely half a dozen buildings which had been erected primarily for the purposes of science teaching. Most of the classes attended by older students were held in the mechanics institutes, in mill or factory premises, in elementary schools or chapel buildings. In almost all cases the teachers depended upon the grants from the Department for their remuneration and it was largely owing to the enlightened self-interest of the teachers that the classes owed their existence.[8]

In sum, during its very early years, technical instruction was very much an ad hoc affair dependent for its success on the provision of grants made to teachers on the basis of the examination results of their students. These early technical teachers were engaged in pursuits other than technical teaching for their main source of income. By the end of the nineteenth century, however, the scene had become more familiar with technical schools (or institutes) and polytechnics, educational establishments devoting themselves almost entirely to science and technical instruction. With their establishment a new group of teachers was created; a body of teachers, primarily men, dependent for their livelihood and status on technical instruction as such.

THE DESERVING POOR BOY

From the 1850s, much of the debate about technical education had centred on the interrelated issues of the nature of the instruction to be given (for example, should it be the more theoretical Science and Art examinations on the one hand or more purely trades instruction on the other) and to whom it should be directed. Many in the Technical Education Movement felt that the priority was not so much the instruction of the artisan but that of the professional scientist and technologist. The development of science in Britain, they believed, had for too long depended on the activities of men who, though brilliant, were essentially amateurs. Indeed Cardwell, throughout his work on the social organisation of science in England, presents evidence to support this view. The slow development of applied science in nineteenth century England, he argues, was due to the lack of a body of professional scientists and technologists to promote it. He notes with approval Huxley's evidence to the Royal Commission on Technical Education of 1881, which indicated that whilst we had men of original capacity equal to the Germans, or indeed to anyone else, we had not anything corresponding to the rank and file that they had in Germany. In that country men could make a living as scientists. There were, for example, many teaching posts in the rapidly multiplying universities and technical colleges.[9]

In England, attempts at professional scientific training had been made as early as 1845 with the foundation of the Royal College of Chemistry and later in 1851 with the Royal College of Mines. Progress, however, was painfully slow. For the first ten years, Cardwell tells us, the average number of matriculants from these two colleges combined was only twelve per annum. The average number of mining matriculants was only four per year, an incredibly small number given the predominance of mining in the economy of the time. The number of fully matriculated students from both these colleges remained at between forty and fifty for about twenty years and this was the case despite their lack of rivals, there being little enough applied science in the universities of the day. Indeed, such was the shortage of men highly qualified in science that the Department of Science and Art had had to employ officers of the Royal Engineers to inspect the new science schools since 'you could hardly find a numerous corps of scientific inspectors, at present, except in that particular body'.[10]

On one point, however, all those interested in scientific and technical education agreed and that was that the greatest hindrance to good instruction at whatever level was the parlous state of education in the country generally. For example, Playfair, an eminent leader of the Technical Education Movement, wrote to the Department of Science and Art as early as 1853 that:

> before scientific instruction, either for adults or
> youths can be made permanently successful, it is
> necessary to create a taste for it by infusing it into
> the primary education of those classes to whom a
> secondary instruction in the scientific principles of
> their trade is necessary. Even before [higher
> institutions] can be satisfactorily established, an
> intermediate class of secondary schools would
> appear to be necessary.[11]

The Royal Commission on Technical Instruction (1881-4)
centred around the question of secondary and elementary
education, asserting that there should be more scholarships
and that local authorities should be empowered to establish
and maintain secondary and technical schools, a development which came about with the Technical Instruction Act
of 1889. What good secondary education existed in the
public schools of the day was a hindrance rather than an
asset, the curriculum being largely classical in content.
1868, for example, found Playfair sadly lamenting the total
ignorance of science on the part of the public school boy.
Whilst we had, he said, the excellent Royal School of
Chemistry and the School of Mines, the great mining
industries could not supply more than twenty men a year
capable of benefiting from them.

The last two decades of the century, however, saw the
creation, if by default, of a form of secondary education
which approximated to the sort of intermediate class of
secondary school Playfair wanted to see. These were the
higher grade and organised science schools made possible by
the money available for Department examinations and the
grants from the Technical Instruction Act. This Act's liberal
definition of what constituted technical instruction, which
included almost any subject not strictly classical in nature,
enabled the higher grade schools (in fact tops to the
elementary schools) to give publicly financed education
which was distinctly secondary in level. By the 1890s, the
higher grade schools were successful rivals to many a
private-venture school which had themselves been increasingly compelled to make use of the grants due to serious
lack of funds. However, the higher grade schools did not see
themselves as rivals to the traditional secondary schools,
but as a distinct alternative to them. They believed that the

fee-paying secondary schools should continue with their predominantly classical curriculum leaving them to train the future engineers and scientists. As for the pupils at such schools, they were of a different social background to that of the typical fee-paying, middle-class secondary school. The higher grade schools comprised a much larger proportion of children from more humble origins. Returns made in 1897 showed that 91 per cent of their pupils had entered from the public elementary schools compared with 49 per cent in the grammar schools and whilst the majority of children in the higher grade schools were of lower middle-class origin, these same returns showed that some 34 per cent of their pupils were the children of manual workers. This compared with a figure of only 6.8 per cent for the grammar schools.[12] By the end of the century, then, another important aim of the Technical Education Movement, that of bringing scientific and technical instruction within the reach of all classes in the community, was nearing fulfilment.

More important still, nearly a decade of compulsory elementary education together with the grants and scholarships made available under the Technical Instruction Act had removed the greatest single obstacle to the achievement of the movement's third aim; the development of scientific and technical education above the elementary level which had largely characterised the teaching at night school. The 1880s saw the development of advanced level work both day and evening in the large technical institutes in the North of England, in the London polytechnics and in the university colleges expanding on the basis of newly created science departments. During the period 1880 to 1890, for example, University and King's College, London, were responsible for 138 Bachelor of Science honours degrees, the provincial university colleges for 219 and Oxbridge for only 56. Other London colleges (that is, primarily the polytechnics) were responsible for no less than 127.[13] Such figures as these would seem to support Sidney Webb's boast that 'more than one Provincial City proud of its new "University College" counts fewer systematic day students than a single London Polytechnic. Even the new provincial universities, with all their dignity of charters and chancellors, diplomas and degrees, often do less work of university grade than a London Polytechnic'.[14] But the Fabian, Webb, was even more proud of the fact that:

As education institutions, the London Polytechnics constitute a new and distinct type, in that their work is not confined to any one grade - still less to any one branch of knowledge or to any one sex -but ranges from the Higher Grade Day School for boys and girls of fourteen, up to high University instruction and post-graduate research. It is now possible, in several of these institutions, for a boy or girl to enter after passing the Fifth Standard at the Public Elementary School, to remain in the Polytechnic Day School up to sixteen or seventeen; on leaving school at any age to continue education in any branch of study, in either evening or day classes; to prepare either for manual labour, commerce, the higher ranges of technical science, or the classical curriculum of the University; to qualify for membership of the professional associations or to take a London degree, and finally to specialise in postgraduate investigation or research, in various departments of science, literature or art.[15]

The large proportion of children from the 'poorer classes' attending the London polytechnics was partly due to the level of work carried out in these institutions and partly due to the low fees and scholarships made possible by the grants to technical education over the last two decades of the century. All scholarships were subject to low parental income (or at least income low enough so as not to compete with the more traditional fee-paying forms of education) and it seems that these scholarships did indeed have the effect of opening up educational opportunities to classes in the community who hitherto would not have enjoyed any education beyond the elementary stage. Of five Senior County Scholarships awarded in London in 1895, for example, three of the scholars pursued engineering, two the natural sciences. Three out of these five had begun their education in the elementary schools and, we are told, would have remained there had it not been for the scholarships. There were 348 applicants for the Board's offer of 30 Intermediate Scholarships in 1894 and of the fifty appointed only six had parents with an income above £250. Thirty had begun their education in elementary schools.[16]

But the London polytechnics were not the only colleges to benefit from these monies. if anything, the school boards in the North of England, under the influence of Liberals of the radical tradition, were more conscientious in their aid to technical education. Senior County Scholars in the North generally attended Owen's College, Manchester where despite the fact that advanced technical classes during the day comprised the major part of the work, evening classes for some 700 students covered exactly the same ground. Again, fees were low and 'the college evening classes especially aimed to serve as an excellent supplement to ordinary science teaching ... in the Board Schools, placing a high standard of instruction within the reach of all in the district'.[17] The Mechanics Institute at Keighley was not untypical of the type of day school that could flourish with the help of grants from the Department of Science and Art. Whilst evening teaching was of such a high standard that the sons of leading manufacturers in the district would attend, the fees were so low that artisans comprised two-thirds of the pupils, the cleverest of these achieving Exhibitions for day technical instruction. In addition, at Keighley, as indeed throughout South Lancashire and the West Riding, 'the deserving poor boy is admitted from elementary school to Trade School for two years free of cost. He may then be retained for another two years and then has the opportunity of winning further Exhibitions to South Kensington where he receives the highest scientific instruction.'[18] By the end of the century, fifty such Exhibitions had been achieved by pupils from Keighley alone.

It was the need of such establishments for more highly qualified teachers of technical subjects and the grants which were made available to their students to train as teachers at South Kensington that gave the real impetus to the birth of technical teaching as a profession. The need for qualified teachers had long been apparent and as early as 1853 the Science and Art Department had recommended:

the creation in the Metropolis of a school of the highest class capable of affording the best instruction and the most perfect training, which could only be hoped for from an institution which had the command of the most eminent and distinguished talent, the advantages of which will be experienced throughout the kingdom, not only as furnishing a central source of information but also as a means of providing well-qualified teachers for local institutions.[19]

The colleges at South Kensington (including the Royal College of Chemistry and the Royal School of Mines) were reorganised to meet this need in 1881, mainly with money from the City and Guilds. From that time on there was a sudden and sharp rise in the number of applicants for admission. The number of government-aided students rose from 25 in 1872 to 94 in 1885 when there were also 136 fee-paying students. In 1895 there were 189 government-aided students compared with 119 fee-payers.[20]

The philosophy underlying the increasing proportion of government-aided to fee-paying students was outlined by the College itself in 1898:

> The Royal College is an institution to supply systematic instruction in the various branches of Physical Science to students of all classes. While it is primarily intended for the instruction of teachers, and of students of the Industrial Classes selected by competition in the examinations of the Science and Art Department, other students are admitted so far as there may be accommodation for them, on the payment of fees fixed at a scale sufficiently high to prevent undue competition with institutions which do not receive state-aid.[21]

Whilst the extent to which able and ambitious students from 'the industrial classes' were able to take advantage of such opportunities should not be exaggerated (scholarships were neither numerous nor generous in these early years) it was generally acknowledged that the government-aided trainee teacher whether at South Kensington or, from 1890, at the University Day Training Colleges where many would-be teachers could read for the London University external degree, were of more modest means than the students who had hitherto had a virtual monopoly of secondary and higher education. It was estimated that in 1898 three-quarters of government-aided students at the Royal College of Science became teachers.

It seems likely, then, that a significant proportion of teachers who joined together in the early twentieth century to form The Association of Teachers in Technical Institutions were from relatively modest social backgrounds. Products of the elementary rather than the more privileged secondary school tradition and the recipients of scholarships, there seems little doubt that many would have come up the hard way. Returns in the early part of the century indicate that there were some 1,470 full-time teachers in post in 97 technical institutes and a further 32,076 part-time teachers spread over no less than 5,933 institutions.[22] About one-fifth of the full-time teachers would have been craft-level teachers who had learnt the principles of their trade at night school. A further fifth had worked in industry at levels higher than that of the artisan and had come to full-time teaching via part-time teaching in the night schools. The remainder had a university degree or equivalent qualifications and taught mainly advanced-level work in the large technical institutes and polytechnics. Some amongst this latter group were ex-elementary teachers who had come to technical teaching through evening classes or university training schemes and who had read for the London University external degree part-time. Others were graduates of South Kensington or the northern University Day Training Colleges.

Whilst not all of the most highly-qualified technical teachers would have been scholarship holders, there are many reasons to suppose that most of them were. Firstly, few fee-payers would have become teachers since they were, in the main, the sons of manufacturers learning the principles of the family trade. Secondly, the few fee-payers who did find their way into teaching would have been both more attracted to the traditional secondary schools, and more likely to be selected by them given the intense competition amongst graduates for educational posts at the turn of the century and a strong preference for candidates who conformed to the Oxbridge pattern. Baron argues strongly that at this time the status of a school varied in inverse proportion to the degree of subsidisation from public funds[23] and on this criterion alone, the secondary schools would have been more attractive to those 'qualified' to teach in them. But status was not the only advantage to be gained from secondary school teaching. In 1908, the ATTI itself complained that university qualified science graduates were going into secondary rather than technical teaching because of the better pay and conditions prevalent there and some time later the Board of Education described conditions in the technical schools and colleges as 'actively distasteful to teachers who have known the amenities of study in a university and cannot but actively repel those students, at least, who have had recent experience of the secondary modern schools.'[24] Given all these factors, it is likely that

13

those teachers who were themselves more purely a product of the technical education movement would have concentrated in the technical colleges themselves.

The upward mobility of many early members of the profession is confirmed by other observations. For example, 80 per cent of the technical teachers who formed the London branch of the ATTI in 1904 were from either South Lancashire or the West Riding, areas where the provision of technical instruction through grants and scholarships had been early and the most well-developed. More qualitative evidence is provided in the many references to leading members of the profession found in the early pages of the Technical Journal, the official journal of the ATTI. Professor Knox, for example, past president and member of the Executive Committee of the Association over many years had started his career in the mines at the age of twelve. Principal Blakeman, a native of Oldham, began his working life as an elementary school part-timer. 'Through sheer grit and determination', however, he acquired a post in a local drawing office from where, via study at evening classes, he gained a scholarship to Owen's College, Manchester and then to Cambridge. Another past president, James Clark, started his educational career as a pupil-teacher in charge of a class of 73 at the age of 13. He studied for a degree at day training college and went on to South Kensington where he became a pupil of Huxley. From there he went to a German university where he was awarded a Doctor of Science to return to England and a post as principal of Truro Technical College after a period of research in Geneva. Mr. Hall, past president and a head of department, also owed his success to the provisions for teacher training. He started his career as a pupil-teacher at the age of twelve but having attended Chester Training College he took up a post in a technical institute where, 'more for the honour of the department than for any other reason', he studied privately for a London external degree. Quite obviously, then, technical teaching provided an avenue of upward mobility for ambitious students of modest means, as did elementary school teaching before it.

Paradoxically, however, it is to the class definitions of education prevailing in the nineteenth century that we owe the developments of technical education which put secondary and higher education (albeit of a certain type) within the reach of students of more modest means. The examinations of the Department of Science and Art, the foundation upon which further developments were built, were made possible only by the low status of science education, a low status which had come about through the growing stress on applied science rather than pure research and the consequent definition of science as a vocational subject rather than a component of the 'liberal' education which was the hallmark of social privilege. This very definition of scientific studies released them from the objection raised against other forms of higher-level education for the masses, namely, that it would give them ideas above their station in life. State aid was made possible precisely because such classes were originally intended for the poor, the prevailing laissez-faire ideology allowing state aid only in the form of 'poor relief'. As we have seen, it was such ideas as these which made possible the development of the polytechnics, the release of funds by the City Parochial Charities being made on the basis that the work of the polytechnics was conceived as 'rescue work' for the poor.

Such considerations as these are crucial in assessing the status of the technical teacher during these early years. If it is true, as Baron argues, that the status of a school varied in inverse proportion to its subsidisation by public monies and further that the status of the teacher depended less on his qualifications than on the type of school in which he taught, then it seems clear that the status of the technical teacher in the educational world could not have been high. Combine this with the fact that the status of an occupational group at this time depended less on any particular expertise and knowledge and more on the social background of its members, add the integral relationship which technical education had with trade and industry (activities despised by the 'professional gentleman') and you have the ingredients for a status which would have been very marginal indeed!

THE HEGEMONY OF THE SECONDARY TRADITION

Despite its modest beginnings, however, it seemed to many that the case for technical education had been won by the end of the century. There had been a rapid development in evening classes at both elementary and higher levels; there was a considerable amount of day work in the higher grade and organised science schools at secondary level and a movement towards full-time advanced studies in the large technical institutes, polytechnics and new university colleges. In addition, a scheme for training technical teachers to the highest level had been instituted. Indeed, such was the influence of the various provisions for technical instruction on education generally that the closing years of the century found the Association of Assistant Masters, the organisation representing teachers in the traditional secondary schools, complaining that 'those who preach the necessity of a sound literary groundwork are still as voices crying in the wilderness'.[26]

By this time, however, the rapid expansion of technical education was already producing the inevitable backlash. Britain had suffered defeats in the Boer War and serious trade competition with Germany. The new applied science was not the panacea it had been thought to be. To the question as to why such endeavour had 'failed', many saw the answer lying in the inadequate provision of secondary education. We had elementary education and technical education, ironically now more than had the Germans. It was believed that the technical education movement had failed to diffuse a knowledge of science amongst the people who really mattered - the leaders of the nation, men in government, the captains of industry, the Civil Service. Others believed it was not instruction which was needed but research; this they considered the most powerful instrument of education there was.

Those directly concerned with technical education would not have disagreed with these arguments as such. For example, a report of the Technical Education Board of the London County Council set up to inquire into the failure of particular London industries to compete abroad ably summed up the deficiencies. As Cardwell notes, this failure to compete, they thought, was due to four specific causes:

1. Lack of scientific training of manufacturers resulted in inability to understand the value of science.

2. Bad secondary education meant that few were really fit to receive advanced technical education.

3. An insufficient supply of young men properly trained in science and in the techniques of applied science.

4. An absence of a higher technical institution sufficiently well-endowed to enable it to give adequate attention to postgraduate and advanced work.[27]

But the worst deficiency of all, they believed, lay in the

area of secondary education:

> In the majority of secondary schools the curriculum
> has been so hamstrung by the exigencies of the
> examining authorities and of examinations, that
> the teacher has been compelled to devote undue
> attention to storing the minds of the students with
> facts for reproduction at the expense of time
> which should be devoted to their reflective powers
> and making them think. In after life [sic!] those
> who enter upon industrial pursuits too often regard
> science with distrust, and to some extent this
> distrust is merited, owing to the insufficient pre-
> paration and training of those who offer them-
> selves for responsible posts in scientific
> industries.[28]

Many of these criticisms were in fact justified. The
curriculum of the higher grade and organised science
schools, whilst secondary in level, was rigid and crammed.
Members of the National Association for the Advancement
of Technical Education, an important champion of technical
instruction founded in 1886, had long been active critics of
the system of payment-by-results, quoting in support of
their arguments appalling examples of rote learning in boys
who had no fewer than eighteen or nineteen passes in
Department examinations. Neither were the teachers totally
happy. 'It is well nigh impossible,' reported The School World
in 1900, 'to carefully study the work of any large technical
institution and not come across a statement by the principal
or one of the teachers concerning the deplorable lack of
general education amongst the students.'
    Indeed, in theory, the technical teachers had everything
to gain from the development of advanced technical education on the basis of a more general secondary education. In
practice, however, it soon became apparent that far from
representing a progression in the status of technical education, the extension of secondary education and the new
emphasis on advanced scientific work represented a threat,
for they came to embody not a radical redefinition of the
nature of technical education as such but a reassertion of
the old class ideas which had governed the theory, if not
always the practice, of education during the whole of the
nineteenth century.
    It seemed at first that the battle of interests over the

nature and extent of provision at secondary level was to be fought out between the secondary and the elementary teachers. With the development of the higher grade schools, the secondary schools had found themselves in direct competition with the elementary schools which, by providing secondary education (of a sort) out of public funds, were threatening their very livelihood. In consequence, the 1890s saw growing agitation by those concerned with secondary education proper for the development of a separate system of secondary education, publicly funded, but staffed, of course, by the traditional secondary teachers. In their eyes, Beatrice Webb tells us, the elementary teacher could not be expected to maintain the high standard of general culture necessary for a genuine secondary education. They believed that genuine secondary education could not as a rule:

> be given by teachers, however industrious or sharp-witted, who came from working-class or lower middle-class homes, who had never enjoyed the advantage of outdoor sports or games or a culti-vated leisure, and who had concentrated their energies from an early age upon the acquisition of the technique of instructing large clases of undis-ciplined children in multifarious subjects. The accent, the manner, the expression, even the physical characteristics and the clothes of the elementary teacher were compared adversely with the more attractive personal characteristics resul-ting from a well-to-do home and the ordinary public school and university education.[29]

As far as the secondary teachers were concerned, the elementary teachers should stick to elementary education, such education continuing to be for the mass of the working class with a liberal provision of scholarships for especially bright pupils who were to be selected for secondary educa-tion at the age of eleven. In short, the policies of the secondary teachers were but a logical extension of what Olive Banks has termed the 'caste-ridden' values which pervaded the educational world of the day.

Needless to say, the elementary teachers were not in accord. For reasons both educational and self-interested, their ideal was one of an:

> all-embracing system of public education from the

infant school to the modernised university, administered by one ad hoc elected authority, regulated by one central Government Department, and served by a homogeneous body of salaried men and women, disciplined by one type of training and belonging to one professional organisation.[30]

They were interested in a totally meritocratic system of education where posts, at whatever level, were thrown open and promotion was 'exclusively by merit, measured not by the social antecedents or previous educational advantages of the candidates, but by their personal character and their ascertained professional and technical qualifications'.[31] In this ideal of one homogeneous educational service there was to be, above all, no distinction between the education of the working-class and of the middle-class child; the school life of the ordinary child was to be significantly extended and wherever the child showed sufficient capacity for higher technical or university education this was to be provided in every case without cost to the parent.

As such, the outcome of this battle need not have affected the technical teachers (except symbolically, of course, in so far as they were themselves of the elementary tradition now under attack) as long as the secondary education to be provided paid sufficient attention to scientific and technical subjects. It seemed at first that this would be the case with the handing over intact of the higher grade and organised science schools to the newly created local authorities in the 1902 Education Act. Earning a grant under the Division A regulations of the Board of Education, these schools were to retain their predominantly scientific and technical character. This was not to be for long, however. Resurgent fears as to an over-emphasis on science and the consequent neglect of more literary subjects caused a radical re-orientation of Board policy as soon as 1903. New regulations were issued which had the effect of destroying the Division A schools as they had come to be known and which reasserted in the new-born, state-subsidised secondary education system, the classical tradition against which the technical teachers had fought so long. As Millis sadly recounts, 'from about 1903 the ordinary secondary schools were allowed to squeeze out of existence the secondary schools of the Division A type and they gradually disappeared'.[32]

Such developments should have come as no surprise to

the technical teachers. In the 1890s, it was becoming apparent that powerful interest groups were pressing not only for secondary education but, under the leadership of the newly formed secondary teachers' associations, against technical teaching as such. For example, the Lockwood Bill, which came out of the Royal Commission on Secondary Education of 1895, proposed to separate secondary from technical education by creating new local authorities to be responsible for secondary education only. Funds were to be provided for secondary education not by instituting new grants but by taking away most of the money made available to technical education under the Local Taxation Act (the 'whisky money'). Even before this, the associations of secondary teachers had pressed for representatives of university and secondary education on the local technical education committees and whisky money had already begun to be devoted to 'not merely haphazard technical classes, but also to the systematic development of scholarships and secondary schools'.[33] Yet whilst the Department of Science and Art, the technical education committees and the school boards remained intact, the technical teachers could feel reasonably safe that the interests of technical as opposed to traditional secondary education would be protected.

In 1900, however, the Department of Science and Art was merged with a new Board of Education to be responsible for all forms of education. It was the avowed aim of the secondary teachers to make the Board, 'unassailably strong, seeing that technical education can take care of itself'.[34] The process of dismantling the administrative machinery which had served technical education so well during the latter half of the nineteenth century was completed with the 1902 Education Act which replaced the school boards and their technical education committees with local education authorities whose brief it was to have responsibility for all forms of education other than elementary. Given the prevailing educational climate and the class influence the secondary teachers' associations had on the various consultative committees set up under the new Act, the technical teachers could no longer be sure that technical education could take care of itself. Indeed, it was the need for representation after the 1902 Education Act, compounded by an unfriendly educational climate that provided the impetus to organisation amongst technical teachers, determining the founding in 1904 of The Association of Teachers in Technical Institutions to make the case for technical education, technical teaching and technical teachers.

A NATION OF CLERKS
The technical teachers were in fact proved right in their fear that developments in the field of secondary education after the 1902 Education Act would render technical education 'a forgotten sector'.

At local as well as national level, the priority lay in the field of secondary education. As the Board itself reported in 1909:

> Great as was the impulse which the Education Act of 1902 gave to higher education generally, its effect on technical education was in practice largely counteracted by the immediate demands which Local Education Authorities found themselves compelled to meet in respect of the long-neglected requirements in their areas of Secondary Schools and the training of teachers. In some districts the reduction then made in the amount of pecuniary support given to technical education has not yet been made good.[35]

Neither could the colleges rely on student demand to make a case for them. The following year, the Board reported that of the 750,000 students enrolled in the evening schools at the time, 20 per cent had failed to complete enough attendances for the local education authorities to make any grants for them. Furthermore, the amount of advanced technical instruction remained 'disappointingly small' and in several institutions, the report tells us, well-qualified staff and excellent equipment stood idle in the day time through lack of students. At this point, the number of day students stood at 8,000, divided equally between full and part-time modes of instruction. This figure grew slowly, rising to 14,700 in 1913 and 22,000 in 1922. Immediately prior to the Second World War there were just over 40,000 day students in the technical colleges. Where evening-only students were concerned, the growth rate was even less, rising, for example, from 867,000 in 1921 to just over a million in 1937.

It is generally agreed that one of the major reasons for this comparative lack of growth was the lack of demand on the part of industry for technically qualified manpower.[36] Several government reports on technical education in the inter-war years bemoaned the comparative indifference to

21

the value of technical education on the part of the employer. In 1926, for example, The Malcolm Committee pointed to 'a disquieting indifference on the part of many employers to the desirability of securing the best possible training for young workers',[37] and the final report of The Balfour Committee (1929) believed that 'nothing less than a revolution' was needed in the outlook of British industry on the question of scientific research.[38] One reason for this lack of appreciation of the importance of science in industry might well have been that few scientists and technologists found themselves in the upper echelons of industry and were therefore in no position to influence policy. But this in itself was merely a reflection of the low status of scientific and technical education during the period in question. Certainly scientific and technical qualifications were no ticket to promotion. Research both pre- and post-war would seem to indicate that the route to top management positions rested firmly within the secondary school tradition, an arts degree from Oxbridge and attendance at a major public school being the two major criteria for promotion.

Another motor for expansion in technical education, that of student demand, was also limited during this period for precisely the same reasons. The low status of science and technology within both the education system and the world of work meant that ambitious parents and pupils looked to the academic curriculum of the grammar schools and the universities for their education. The whole ethos of Edwardian England was directed towards respectable white-collar jobs. A measure of this demand can be seen in the increase in professional and commercial day classes in the technical colleges during the inter-war years. The proportion of full-time day classes specifically related to industry fell from 84 per cent of the total in 1913 to 59 per cent in 1937. On the other hand, the proportion of professional and commercial classes rose from 11 per cent to 27 per cent during the same period. The remaining full-time day classes were made up of more general subjects, for example mathematics and general science, English and foreign languages at matriculation level, again an indication of the pull of the white-collar world as matriculation was highly regarded as the key to entry prior to the Second World War. Professional and commercial evening classes had long exceeded classes in industrial subjects. In 1911, for example, the relative proportions stood at some 21 and 11 per cent of the total. By 1937, however, the gap had narrowed somewhat, the relative proportions standing at some 20 and 15 per cent respectively.

There was, then, little advance to speak of during the inter-war years. The growth in absolute numbers was steady but slow and the proportion of day technical classes, whether full or part-time remained but a minute proportion of the total, rising from 2.5 per cent in 1921 to but 3.5 per cent in 1937. It is not with exaggeration, therefore, that Richardson, in his contemporary account of the organisation of technical education before the Second World War, asserted that the technical college remained still a night school. Evening-only work had obvious disadvantages for the students, who, if following one of the many grouped courses, would have to attend college on three nights a week. That this was too much for many after a full day's work was apparent from the higher wastage rates which the Board of Education continually reported. Neither were the more progressive industrialists totally unaware of the problem. Richardson, for example, quotes the President of the Institution of Production Engineers who, in his address of 1937, stated that 'to ask, or even to expect, the youth of today to spend three nights per week, plus homework, after his day's work, is approaching very nearly to exploitation'.[39] And at advanced level, the part-time evening nature of the work combined with the inflexibility of the London University external degree examination system led to not unjustifiable accusations that the colleges were mere 'cramming institutions', force-feeding students just enough information to get by.

In view of such considerations as these, it is important to consider the one reform during this period which might have had a significant effect on the quality, if not necessarily the quantity, of work achieved in the technical colleges. This was the development after 1921 of the National Certificate Schemes. After the abolition of pay-ment-by-results in 1906, the examinations had continued in similar form until 1911 when the Board of Education proposed that 'grouped courses' should be developed at non-advanced level in co-operation with the teachers in the colleges. The aim was to overcome the unsystematic knowledge acquired by students taking examinations in many often unrelated subjects and to enable staff to develop such courses by freeing them from an extremely rigid external examination system. After the First World War, the Board became anxious that this should also apply to more advanced work and the colleges were consequently invited to frame curricula and syllabuses for a three nights a week course to extend over two or three years of study. Examinations were to be internal, subject only to external assessment in the final year. A form of continuous assessment was also to be introduced and attendance requirements would have to be met. So few schemes were forthcoming from the colleges, however, that the Board itself had to take the initiative and after approaching the professional associations for assistance a plan was put forward to issue joint certificates along the above lines. The resulting system of National Certificates could be studied either full or part-time and would cover two levels of work, the ordinary and the higher - roughly equivalent to technician and technologist levels respectively.

The scheme grew slowly but steadily, the number of passes awarded rising, for example, from 2,792 in 1931 to 5,330 in 1939. But these figures obscure the fact that from the start the part-time mode of study was much more popular than the full-time, and that at the higher level at least, those students in a position to study full-time would prefer to do so at a university.[40] As we shall see, then, as now, the university degree had a status which was difficult to beat, no matter how illustrious the originators of an alternative!

NOTES

1. D.S.L. Cardwell, The Organisation of Science in England (Heinemann, 1957), p.59.

2. F.E. Foden, 'A History of Technical Examinations in England to 1918: With Special Reference to the City and Guilds of London Institute', unpublished PhD thesis, University of Reading, 1961.

3. C.T. Millis, Technical Education, Its Development and Aims (Arnold, 1925), p.28.

4. Cardwell, The Organisation of Science, p.102.

5. Ibid. p.100.

6. H.C. Dent, Part-time Education in Great Britain (Turnstile Press, 1949), pp.17-18.

7. Millis, Technical Education, pp.29-30.

8. Board of Education, Annual Report, 1900-1901, vol.2, p.248.

9. Cardwell, The Organisation of Science, p.106.

10. Quoted in ibid. p.89.

11. Quoted in ibid. p.71.
12. Olive Banks, Parity and Prestige in English Secondary Education (Routledge & Kegan Paul, 1955), p.29.
13. Cardwell, The Organisation of Science, p.129.
14. Sidney Webb, London Education (Longmans, 1904), p.162.
15. Ibid. pp.146-7.
16. For details of this early provision in technical education see The Record, journal of the National Association for the Promotion of Secondary Education.
17. The Record, vol.V, p.425.
18. Ibid. p.320.
19. Millis, Technical Education, p.35.
20. Cardwell, The Organisation of Science, p.124.
21. Quoted in Millis, Technical Education, p.36.
22. Statistics of Public Education in England and Wales, 1906.
23. G. Baron, 'The Secondary Schoolmaster, 1895-1914', unpublished PhD thesis, University of London, 1952.
24. Survey of Technical and Further Education in England and Wales (Board of Education, 1926), p.26. This pamphlet also contains a useful summary of provision from 1825 onwards.
25. A graphic example of the low status of the early technical teachers employed by the Department of Science and Art is given by Foden when he describes the military influence in the Department. Many of the officials were high-ranking officers in the Royal Engineers or the Navy and, Foden tells us, dealt with the teachers 'as though they were infantry privates, not paid to think, probably unable to think anyway, and unlikely to have motives much higher than the desire for mere gain'. In consequence, 'no arrangements were ever made for taking the opinions of the rank and file into account ... All decisions were passed down as commands from the top, there was no traffic of consultation the other way'. Foden, 'Technical Examinations', pp.146-7.
26. Quoted in Banks, Parity and Prestige, p.32.
27. Cardwell, The Organisation of Science, p.156.
28. Quoted in ibid. pp.150-1.
29. Mrs Sidney Webb, 'English Teachers and their Professional Organization', Special Supplement in New Statesman, vol.V, 25 September 1915, p.20.
30. Ibid. p.19.
31. Ibid.
32. Millis, Technical Education, p.99.

33. The proponents of traditional secondary education were having a great deal of success in pressing their point of view during the last decade of the century. For example, Mrs Sidney Webb tells us that 'owing to the fact that the leading members of the Headmasters' Association and Headmasters' Conference belonged to the same social class as the Cabinet Ministers, the Chief Permanent Officials, and the majority of Members of Parliament, and had, in fact, been their tutors and headmasters, they had easy access to them in unofficial and informal ways'. Their persistent agitation led to the setting up of a Royal Commission in 1894 to consider 'the best ways of establishing a well-organised system of secondary education in England'. Mrs Webb claims that this Commission was to an extraordinary degree 'packed' with members steeped in the social and educational ideals of the public schools and the two older universities. Mrs Widney Webb, New Statesman, 1915.

34. Quoted in Banks, Parity and Prestige, p.32.

35. Board of Education, Annual Report 1909, pp.68-9. All the statistics describing the period up to 1944 are from the Board of Education Annual Reports unless otherwise stated. Of the period up to the Education Act of 1944, the Editor of the Technical Journal, official journal of the ATTI, had this to say: 'there is no doubt from the debate which took place on the 1902 Education Bill that everyone expected there would be a substantial measure of Technical Education. What happened? The Board immediately defined secondary education in such a way as virtually to exclude any Technical Education whatsoever. When the Junior Technical Schools at last forced recognition from the Board they were hedged around by regulations that deliberately made them a dead-end. They were forbidden to plan courses which would lead to University, to the Professions, or indeed to full-time Technical Education itself. For at least 30 years no technician or technologist ... has occupied a position of responsibility on the Board's hierarchy. A technical department was formed but immediately starved. It took a world war to get the first penny, but the history of the years since the last war carry on the same terrible story.'

36. See, for example, Stephen Cotgrove, Technical Education and Social Change (Allen & Unwin, 1958); M. Argles, South Kensington to Robbins (Longmans, 1964); T. Burgess & J. Pratt, Policy and Practice (Allen Lane, 1970).

37. Report of the Committee on Education and Industry

(Malcolm Committee, 1926). Quoted in Cotgrove, <u>Technical Education and Social Change</u>, p.77.

38. <u>Report of the Committee on Industry and Trade</u> (Balfour Committee, 1929). Quoted in Cotgrove, <u>Technical Education and Social Change</u>, p.84.

39. Quoted in W.A. Richardson, <u>The Technical College, Its Organisation and Administration</u> (Oxford University Press, 1939), p.472.

40. See Burgess & Pratt, <u>Policy and Practice</u>, p.19 ff for details of provision in both the universities and the technical colleges during this period.

2

The Era of Expansion

A UNIVERSAL PROCESS OF ASPIRATION

Such was the relative success of the part-time Higher National Certificate that by the time of the Percy Report, Higher Technological Education, in 1945, it was found that more civil, electrical and mechanical engineers were being produced by the technical colleges than by the universities, the number of certificates to degrees standing at 1,300 and 1,250 respectively.[1] It was in fact the publication of the Percy Report which heralded the great debate about the provision of advanced scientific and technological education which dominated the years following the Second World War. The report identified the two major sources of provision; the universities with their more general and academic degrees and the technical colleges with their more vocationally oriented certificates. In addition, the technical colleges were also making a significant contribution to the awarding of degrees, the London polytechnics awarding internal degrees of the University and the major technical colleges outside London awarding its external degree. The courses in the technical colleges were followed on a predominantly part-time basis, the vast majority of the students attending in the evening after a full day's work. The universities, on the other hand, for the most part insisted on full-time study, preferably residential after the monastic tradition of the older universities. Entrance requirements for technical college qualifications were flexible; in theory, at least, the skilled craftsman with only an elementary education could work his way up through the City and Guilds craft-level courses to the Ordinary National Certificate and then on to the Higher National Certificate which was considered to be of ordinary degree standard. The universities, on the other hand, continued to insist on matriculation in the tradition of the academic grammar school. As we shall see, it can be argued that the post-war expansion in public sector further and higher education was at least in part the product of the academic exclusiveness of the universities.

The Percy Report was set up explicitly to advise on 'the needs of higher technological education in England and Wales and the respective contributions to be made thereto by the Universities and the Technical Colleges'.[2] It recommended that each type of institution should continue to make a contribution but stressed that the major contribution of the technical colleges lay in the provision of technical assistants and draughtsmen rather than of scientists and technologists who should be trained predominantly in the universities. The part-time mode of study would continue to be adequate for two-thirds of technical college students, though the report preferred part-time day to evening-only study. For the remaining third of technical college students, the report recommended the development of degree-level courses on what has now become known as the 'sandwich' principle - that is continuous full-time study interleaved with industrial placement. However, such courses were to be developed in only a small number of technical colleges which were to change significantly in character. They were to have a considerable number of residential students, adequate governing bodies and staff representation on academic boards. They were to be to a large degree centrally financed and the pay and conditions of their staff were to resemble those of university teachers. To enable them to create the right kind of 'academic atmosphere', they were to concentrate on higher-level work and drop lower-level teaching. Furthermore, there was to be a new qualification equivalent in status and prestige to the university honours degree. About the title of the award, however, there was some disagreement. Some, particularly those who wanted to raise the status of technological education, recommended that the award should be called a degree. Others, concerned to maintain the symbolic purity of the traditional university degree, proposed that it be called a diploma. Lord Eustace Percy himself recommended the setting up of a Royal College of Technology which would confer Associateships at undergraduate level, Fellowships at postgraduate level. But whichever, it seemed that here at last was the sort of high-status technological institution of which the proponents of technical education had dreamed since the beginning of the Technical Education Movement in the last century.

Such recommendations as were embodied in the Percy Report were not to be implemented, and then only partially, until after the publication of the 1956 White Paper on technical education. In the meantime, however, there was without doubt movement in what was increasingly known as the further education sector. At the institutional level, a permanent pressure group was set up in the form of the National Advisory Council on Education for Industry and Commerce (NACEIC) in 1947. The following year saw Regional Advisory Councils (RACs) established to co-ordinate provision, especially in the more advanced spheres. Student demand increased significantly at both advanced and non-advanced levels. In 1950, for example, the number of students working for external London degrees on a full-time basis stood at 8,772 and on a part-time basis at 11,295 and this figure did not include the large number of students who were following degree courses on an evening-only basis. The colleges had grown, and were still growing, to accommodate large numbers of servicemen leaving the forces and taking advantage of the government grants made available to them to study. The colleges took 10,882 such students in 1950, 5,756 of whom studied applied science and 4,755 pure. Their numbers were almost evenly divided between full and part-time study. As Burgess and Pratt remark, 'This taste of advanced work in so many subjects gave the technical colleges, some for the first time, a new view of their own possibilities and a new ambition for development.'[3]

Again, on the surface at least, it seemed as if the future of higher education within the further education sector was assured. Official reports of the day were full of the 'substantial contribution' made by the colleges to the training of technologists.[4] In 1951, a White Paper was published which accepted proposals put forward by the NACEIC for a Royal College of Technologists. Furthermore, the local authorities were to receive a 75 per cent grant in respect of advanced work instead of the 60 per cent main education grant. A change of government, however, saw the proposals for a special award dropped although the provision for a 75 per cent grant was put into effect. The number of applications for recognition under this arrangement was a measure of the ambition of both the colleges and the local authorities in respect of the provision of advanced-level work. In 1953, the Board of Education had approved 382 courses at 20 technical colleges. During the course of 1954, the number of approved courses rose by 113 to 495 and the number of colleges in receipt of the grant to 24. By the end of that year, local education authorities had sought approval for no less than 1,300 courses in over 92 different colleges.[5]

Closer reflection might have indicated, however, that its future was still uncertain. For example, it might have been inferred from the inaction over a Royal College of Technologists that the government of the day was firmly convinced that higher education should not have a permanent place in the technical colleges. There were at the time strong pressures against such a policy coming from the universities and from the Advisory Council on Scientific Policy which in its report of 1949 argued that:

Besides graduates in technology there is an urgent need in industry of an increase in the number of men of the highest quality who have received an education up to university honours standard in pure and applied science. For a variety of reasons we were agreed that the foundations of such an education could only be laid in the universities where teaching and research in the fundamental sciences are carried out ... The primary need is for more men who have reached honours degree standard in fundamental science to be given post-graduate education in applied science. This need can be met in this country only by the universities.[6]

Government policy in the early fifties would seem to indicate that it was more in sympathy with the advice of the Advisory Council than the NACEIC. In 1953, for example, a £15 million expansion of Imperial College was begun and in 1954 a £6 million development programme for the civic universities was announced. This was in addition to the £16 million plus already committed to university expansion since the war, over eighty per cent of which had gone to science and technology.

In part as a consequence of this expansion of science and technology in the universities, the years immediately preceeding the publication of the White Paper in 1956 were uncertain ones for the technical colleges. The number of students undertaking advanced work began to decline. The number of external degrees gained by technical college students dropped from over 500 in 1951 to just over 200 in 1955 and the proportion of full-time degree to other full-time work fell by half during the same period. So the shift in government policy went neither unfelt nor unnoticed in the colleges. The Executive of the ATTI, for example, received several reports from divisions expressing alarm at both the reduced number and quality of students entering degree or degree-level equivalent courses. The Executive, however, considered it inadvisable to publicise these facts as they would detract from the attempts which were being made to raise the status of higher technological education in the technical colleges.

It was not without some relief, therefore, that the colleges greeted the publication of the government White Paper, Technical Education, in 1956. A five-year programme of development in technical and vocational education was announced with proposals to expand the technical college out-put of technologists from the nine and a half thousand trained in 1956 to fifteen thousand in 1961. The White Paper also incorporated one of the most important proposals of the Percy Report, that of developing a technological award equal in status to the university honours degree. This award, the Diploma in Technology (in deference to university interests), was to be developed by the colleges themselves and validated by the National Council For Technological Awards (NCTA) which had been set up the previous year. Again, only a limited number of colleges were to be approved to run such courses. These colleges were to be designated the Colleges of Advanced Technology (CATs) and there was a strong implication that there would be twenty-four, the twenty-four which had been able to take advantage of the government's 75 per cent grant for advanced work over the previous years. Such was not to be the case, however, and in the summer of 1956, the government issued Circular 305 which made it clear that expansion was to be accompanied by rationalisation.

The circular provided for four main types of college defined according to both the level of work taught and the predominant mode of attendance. The Local Colleges were to undertake courses, usually part-time, up to Ordinary National Certificate level. The Area Colleges were to continue with their full-time and sandwich non-advanced level work with some part-time advanced work. The Regional Colleges would continue to make some contribution to the provision of advanced courses on a full-time basis but the great proportion of their work was to be part-time. They would also continue to offer some non-advanced work. The CATs were to have a substantial volume of exclusively advanced work, mainly full-time and sandwich. The names of the types of college implied their catchment area. The CATs, of course, were to be national institutions.

More importantly, there were to be designated only eight (later ten), not twenty-four as was originally implied. Thus it was that there emerged a hierarchy of colleges, each type with its distinctive level of work and predominant mode of attendance. A necessary measure, it might be argued, given that over the immediate post-war years further education had 'like Topsy, just growed'. Many thought that the result had been a wasteful duplication of courses in neighbouring institutions and a patchwork of provision over the country. But this did not make those colleges who were about to lose their advanced-level work any happier, nor those regional colleges which despite their efforts had not been designated CATs.

The 1956 White Paper has been described by many as a landmark in technical education. Not only did it place scientific and technical education firmly on the educational agenda, it also 'legitimised for the first time the development of higher education to university level outside the university'.⁷ Neither was the Diploma in Technology without symbolic significance. Whilst it operated for only ten years (until the CATs became technological universities with powers to award their own degrees) it was the first award of honours degree standard to be validated independently of the universities. On the other hand, it could be argued that implicit in the White Paper's proposals were the old class ideas as to the proper institutions for the training of different ranks of society. There is evidence to suggest, for example, that the reversal of government policy embodied in the White Paper was not so much the product of a whole-hearted commitment to the technical college tradition as of a changed definition of manpower needs on the part of the government and the universities. For as long as both saw the country's manpower needs in terms of the training of a moderate number of technologists at the highest level, there was no question that the proper place for that training was in the universities. However, in the years immediately prior to 1956, the government became convinced (on the basis of somewhat dubious comparisons with other countries) that what was needed was expansion at the intermediate as well as the most advanced levels and that the expansion needed at the most advanced levels was much greater than they had previously envisaged. The government began to doubt, perhaps, whether the universities were willing or able to absorb such large numbers of applied scientists. Burgess and Pratt, for example, argue that, 'the government had plumped for the universities to carry out the major expansion of advanced technological education, but was faced with a slow growth in the numbers of technologists actually coming out of the universities'.[8] 'After all the post-war efforts,' they continue, '31 per cent of all scientists and technologists produced were actually technologists compared with 23 per cent at the time of the Percy Report. The absolute numbers were 1,873 and 1,259 respectively.'[9] The only pragmatic solution was to increase the already considerable amount of advanced work in the technical colleges.

The reaction of the universities to the White Paper would seem to confirm this interpretation. In certain quarters it was welcomed with some relief that they themselves were not going to be subject to pressure to increase their numbers beyond those they believed really capable of a university education. Indeed, one professor of electrical engineering went as far as to suggest that:

> Persons do not exist in these numbers who are capable of being trained in the real university tradition, nor does the country need these vast numbers of people to think at this high intellectual level. The education elsewhere of those who are not aiming at high intellectual standards will safe-guard the position of those who are.[10]

To some it was 'a cause of great satisfaction that the sheer weight of numbers is to be taken elsewhere, enabling the universities to deal with the elite of the engineering profession'.[11] The fate of advanced-level work in the colleges seemed to depend still on what the universities were either willing or able to do. Indeed, the fact that advanced work was not to be spread over the twenty-four regional colleges but was to be concentrated in a small number of CATs was not just a question of rationalisaton. It embodied a whole educational philosophy. Simply put, the CATs were to become as much like universities as possible and this meant especially that they should drop any of their remaining non-advanced work, work which, as Burgess and Pratt tell us, 'was at the time almost universally held to sully the picture'.[12] With the Robbins Report in 1963 they became in name as well as in fact technological universities.

Indeed, with Robbins the policy of shedding non-advanced work was elevated to an educational principle. Robbins wanted to see the number of university places rise from the then existing 119,000 to 350,000 by 1980/1. It was envisaged that the existing universities might provide some 300,000 of these places and six new universities a further 30,000. The remainder was to be provided by a selected number of the regional colleges which had not been designated CATs in the late fifties, and some colleges of education. The selected colleges were to follow the same road as the CATs before them, becoming eventually either universities themselves or constituent colleges of existing universities. The non-designated regional colleges had been disappointed and demoralised at the designation of the eight CATs in 1956. As they saw it, the only alternative left was one of emulation in the hope of future designation. Despite the fact that only one college was successful in pursuing this policy (Brunel was designated a CAT in 1960), such was their determination that in the years between 1958 and 1965, advanced-level work outside the CATs rose by 86 per cent, three times as fast as in the CATs themselves! The number of students on advanced courses outside the CATs stood at 162,380, inside at 19,000. The majority of these students were, of course, following National Certificate courses, though the regional colleges also carried a share of the Diplomas in Technology and the traditional London University external degree. It is understandable, then, that the initial reaction of the colleges to the CATs becoming universities was one of resentment. A measure of their thwarted ambitions was that in the year following the Robbins Report no less than twenty applications were made to the Ministry of Education to fill the projected university vacancies.

Neither were ambitions for up-grading restricted to the disappointed regional colleges. The area colleges in their turn were jealous of their advanced work and, given trends in policy, felt that they needed regional status to secure it. Circular 305 had said that it was not the Minister's intention to fix the list of regional colleges once and for all and area colleges which could fulfil the criteria laid down in the circular were permitted to develop advanced courses. Thus it was that not only the regional but also the area colleges began the drive to shed lower-level work. It is not difficult to imagine the conflict which such a 'universal process of aspiration' as described by Burgess and Pratt might cause in the colleges between staff who stood to gain by such a policy and those who stood to lose. Indeed, one study of an aspiring area college in the mid-sixties suggests that the battle line was drawn between those qualified to teach higher-level work and those who were not. The net result was one of low morale and disunity amongst the staff.[13]

There were to be no new universities, however. In the spring of 1965, Anthony Crosland, the then Secretary of State for Education and Science, elaborated what came to be known as the 'binary policy' in higher education, a policy which was to form the basis of the 1966 White Paper, A Plan for Polytechnics and Other Colleges, and which determined the essential structure of higher education for the next two decades. It has been argued that an assumption underlying much of government policy in higher education in the post-war years was that if, for whatever reason, manpower needs could not be met by the universities, then at least they should be met under conditions closely resembling those of the universities. It was ironic that the development of advanced-level work in the technical colleges and the corresponding establishment of high-status technological institutions, far from strengthening the position of higher education within the further education sector, actually, weakened it. The Colleges of Advanced Technology were 'creamed off' from the public sector and swallowed up by the university tradition. Such would have been the fate of the regional colleges had the Robbins proposals been fully implemented. By way of contrast, the binary policy as propounded by Mr Crosland paid tribute to both the university and technical college traditions and wanted to preserve each with its 'own distinctive contribution to the whole'. In order to do this, the government were to create 30 new polytechnics out of the already existing colleges with a significant proportion of high-level work. These polytechnics, he argued elsewhere, were definitely not to emulate the universities but were to retain some sub-degree work and an emphasis on part-time education. In so doing, he believed that the polytechnics would continue the traditional role of the technical colleges as agents of social mobility. 'What we see as the role of the Polytechnics,' he explained, 'is something distinctive from the universities, and more comprehensive.'[14]

How far such statements as these represented a real belief on the part of the Wilson government as a whole in the value of the technical college tradition is difficult to say. It was certainly argued in some quarters that the binary policy was a matter of economic expediency; that the government faced with a commitment to the Robbins principle that there should be places in higher education for all who were qualified by ability and attainment and who wanted it, saw in the binary idea an opportunity to provide those places 'on the cheap'. But whether or not this was the case, the binary policy was real in its consequences. The total number of students following advanced courses in colleges other than the CATs in England and Wales stood at 162,380 in 1966. By 1968 the figure had risen to 188,100 and by 1973 it stood at 208,320. Of these advanced students, approximately 60 per cent were concentrated in the polytechnics. Again, in 1966, students in the public sector took 1,381 London University degrees and diplomas. By 1973/4, this figure had risen to 3,310. In addition, in that year, 7,370 CNAA first degrees were awarded and 17,385 Higher National Certificates and Diplomas. In comparison, 45,393 first degrees and diplomas were awarded in the universities in England and Wales that year. By 1981, if full-time, part-time and sandwich students are included, the public sector contributed just over half the provision of higher education in the country. On this measure, by 1983, there were 460,700 home students in public sector higher education compared with 370,000 in the universities. But as we shall see, this relative advantage was achieved under conditions very different from those pertaining during the era of expansion.

EDUCATION VS TRAINING

Whilst it might be argued that it was the growth of advanced-level work which had the most significant impact on the changing character of further education during this period, there were also major developments in the provision of non-advanced further education (NAFE). These developments, however, proceeded smoothly in comparison with those at advanced level beset as they were with controversies about the rightful place of higher education in the education system as a whole. There was no such argument about the rightful place of vocational education below advanced level, indeed it was to the traditional provision of such work that the technical colleges owed their low status in the educational world and dubious public image. Even so, it was not until the 1956 White Paper that the official mind turned seriously to the provision of craft and technician education, pre-occupied as it had been with advanced scientific and technical provision. The White Paper had defined three levels of vocational training: technologist, technician and craft. As well as recommending that the number of technologists should double over the following five years, it recommended that there should be a proportionate increase at the other levels as well. There was also concern that day-release should be developed as an alternative to part-time evening-only study and in the years between 1955 and 1961, the number of students released from industry on this basis grew from 355,000 to 681,000, not an insignificant advance given that the government was, at this point, relying totally on the voluntary efforts of the employers.[15]

in 1962 a committee was appointed to suggest ways of achieving the maximum practicable rise in day-release for the under 18 age-group. In its report (Day Release, 1964), the committee recommended that the number of employees under that age attending day-release classes should double from a quarter to half a million by 1969/70. As to how that order of expansion was to be achieved, however, the report remained vague. Educationalists had long argued that for any substantial increase in day-release to occur, it would be necessary to compel either young workers to attend college or their employers to release any employee wishing to attend but the report recommended neither. In 1964, the government published a further White Paper, Better Opportunities in Technical Education, which recommended changes in the structure of City and Guild's courses to help combat wastage and achieve more sensitivity to industrial needs and yet again, the importance of day-release as opposed to evening-only study was singled out.[16]

Both the 1961 White Paper and the 1964 Report (The Henniker-Heaton Report) were also concerned with the continuing education, as well as the vocational training, of the 15-18 age-group. In 1959, the Crowther Report had focussed on the waste involved in the way the English education system allowed the great majority of young people to abandon full-time education on leaving school at the age of 15. As a solution to this problem it had suggested an expansion of further education to accommodate those youngsters who might not desire, or be capable of, the traditional academic approach to post-school education. It was envisaged that further education might provide an 'alternative road', offering a broad liberal education with a practical bias. In effect, Crowther wanted to resurrect the county college proposals embodied in the 1944 Education Act which envisaged that all youngsters would attend college for at least the equivalent of one day a week to undertake 'such further education, as will enable them to develop their various aptitudes and capacities and will prepare them for the responsibilities of citizenship'.[17] The employers were to be obliged to release their employees, one of the reasons, perhaps, why the proposals were quietly dropped during the period of post-war reconstruction.

It was not until the Industrial Training Act was passed in 1964 that the prevailing laissez-faire attitude to the 15-18 age-group was challenged. Briefly, the Act provided for the setting up of industrial training boards empowered to decide on the training needs of their particular industry. Their activities were to be co-ordinated by the Central Training Council. Having decided on the necessary levels of training, the boards were then empowered to impose a levy on all firms within the industry which was then paid back in the form of an industrial training grant on condition that the individual firm fulfil the training requirements laid down by the board. It was hoped that individual firms would train their employees in order to recoup the money paid under the levy, with the additional incentive that the cost of training was now more evenly spread throughout the industry.

A major requirement of the Industrial Training Act was that trainees should receive associated further education in the colleges themselves and the Central Training Council defined its aim as:

> to provide the knowledge and appreciation of techniques necessary for the trainee to do his job; to inculcate a broad understanding of relevant science and technology, so that the trainee appreciates the problems of those working in associated occupations and is also equipped to adjust to changes in the nature of his work; to widen the trainee's understanding of the society in which he lives and the development of his personality; and to prepare suitable trainees for more advanced study leading to more highly skilled work.[18]

Thus whilst this was indeed an industrial training act, training was more broadly defined than the mere instruction of the young worker as to how better to perform his or her particular task. Rather there was to be some education in the wider principles underlying the trade or industry as well as an attempt to include some aspects of a more 'liberal' education. To achieve these aims it was necessary that the young worker be released to attend college.

As such, the Act might have been expected to have a considerable impact on the colleges, but there were limitations. It did not impel employers to release their trainees, merely to pay the levy, and it was often less of a cost to the employer to forfeit the levy than to release the trainee. Further, its provisions were so interpreted as to exclude many youngsters who were in fact trainees. In 1965, for example, the Minister of Labour had stated in Parliament that he would normally only approve proposals from the industrial training boards if they made payment of the training grant conditional upon all young employees receiving day release in occupations requiring a substantial amount of training. The operative word here was substantial. In practice it was interpreted to mean training needs of at least a year's duration, thereby automatically excluding a large proportion of young workers. And even so, a report issued by the Central Training Council in 1969 suggested that up to 40 per cent of those trainees falling within this category were not being released by their empoloyers.[19] As a result, the proportion of young workers released increased but little over the years following the Act, rising but marginally from 19 per cent of the under 18 age-group in 1964/5 to 24 per cent in 1970.

Neither was the Industrial Training Act regarded as an unequivocal bonus by the colleges, even though they had long been calling for compulsory day release. The ATTI feared that the emphasis would be on the training rather than the educational components of the Act, and that with industrial interests so well represented on the industrial training boards, the teachers would be powerless to resist. Another, though related, fear was that the traditional links between industrial training and further education would be weakened rather than strengthened, employers finding it cheaper and more convenient to set up their own training schools rather than send their employees to college. There is evidence to suggest, however, that not all lecturers were over-concerned with such problems. For example, a survey caried out by Ethel Venables in 1962 found that almost half of the staff in the six local technical colleges she studied did not object to rigid external controls.[20] Neither would all lecturers be too worried about the training tail wagging the educational dog. Tipton, for example, reports hostile attitudes to liberal studies on the part of the traditional technical teachers in the area college she studied in the mid-sixties on the very grounds that it interfered too much with vocational training:

> If a firm finds it can release a student only one day a week then in fairness to the student and employers it should be used for technical training ... the employer is paying you to do a particular job, he is not paying you to do liberal studies.
> Senior Lecturer, Management Studies

> Liberal Studies should be utilitarian, English rather than Liberal Studies, not too liberal. It should include things like report writing, letter writing, office procedure and speech training.
> Assistant Lecturer, Science Department[21]

If such was the prevailing climate of opinion within the technical colleges, then the young graduates recruited to teach liberal studies might experience a very severe culture shock.

Venables suggests on the basis of her research in local colleges that such cultural lines could indeed be drawn between ex-school teachers and lecturers recruited from industry who had themselves come up the hard way in the tradition of the technical college. For their part, teachers of liberal studies were sharply critical of what they considered to be a lack of professional attitude towards teaching on the part of those recruited from industry:

> Some staff regard the courses as purely vocational and the Social Studies sessions as 'bull'. I have no patience with them. They look upon the college as a vocational training centre and not as an educational institution.

> Many of the staff came from industry where production is all that matters. This spills over into teaching - getting through the exams is all that matters.[22]

But many staff also complained that the constraints imposed by the system of day-release made it impossible to carry out even the task of vocational training effectively. In one local

41

college studied by Venables, for example, the students had to attend on one day and one evening a week to get through the externally-imposed syllabus. To accommodate the students' reluctance to make the journey to college twice a week, teaching was organised from 9 o'clock in the morning until 9 o'clock at night with virtually no break in between. Complaints from the staff were numerous and bitter:

> It's educationally wrong - learning should be efficient.

> We're just a sausage machine - an annexe to the local factory - people lecturing to them all the time.

> Lots of the work is purely mechanical - a chap may know Ohm's law but not know anything about it.[23]

Such conditions as these combined with the difficulties of building up rapport with large numbers of students a lecturer might see for only an hour or two once a week go a long way to explaining the high wastage rates on many of these courses. They might also help explain the striving of many lecturers after higher-level work. Apart from any status considerations, the job satisfaction would be so much greater.

In sum, the era of expansion was not without its problems for many in the colleges. The colleges were simultaneously under threat from three directions. At one end of the spectrum, what advanced work they were engaged in was in continual danger of being 'creamed off', first by the regional colleges, then by the polytechnics. At the other end of the spectrum, developments in industrial training were threatening the integrity of much college-based, craft-level work and the prospect of the raising of the school leaving age and the development of the sixth-form college had implications for GCE 'A' level courses in the further education sector. Added to all this, progressive rationalisation raised the spectre of re-deployment (even redundancy) for some, reduced career prospects for others. A measure of the degree of rationalisation which was taking place during this period can be taken from the fact that in 1966 there were some 705 major establishments and 25 regional colleges; by 1971, there were 636 major establishments and thirty polytechnics and by 1974, there were 564 major establishments with no increase in the number of polytechnics.

Rationalisation on such a scale obviously caused problems. The individual colleges which were to merge had their own distinctive histories, styles of management and staff relationships. An extreme example was that of one newly-created London polytechnic where the problems surrounding the appointment of a director were greatly exacerbated by shifting alliances and conflicts among the staff. Again the lines seemed to have been drawn between the attitudes and values of the technical college tradition and the more 'liberal' wind of change which had been blowing in the sixties. For example, one of the colleges to be merged was described as:

> a stable, slightly old-fashioned college run by well-qualified capable staff; an institution which had many long-standing links with industry, professional bodies, and other colleges and universities, and which ran well-established courses based on considerable experience. Compared with many other colleges, the staff were older and had been longer in the same college. They were content to plough their own furrows, were hard-working and conservative, and largely unwilling to consider new courses or new ideas unless forced by lack of students or by external pressures ... The change-over to CNAA degrees was regarded as probably inevitable, but a move to be fought off and delayed as long as possible.[25]

Science and technology dominated the colleges and there had been little growth or diversity since the war. In addition, the real units of government were the departments which 'were strong centres of power ruled often by heads who were both competent and used to getting their own way'.

In contrast, the late fifties and sixties were a period of continuous expansion and development at the other college and by the time of the merger, the bias was towards the arts and social sciences. Its growth had not been steady and evolutionary and:

> The Principal was preoccupied with the status of the college and with expansion, especially

> expansion into areas of higher-level work ... He collected about him in senior positions a group of like-minded persons. The particular mixture of specialisms finally settled on ... comes mostly from those being most in demand in the late fifties and sixties. If there was a strong but unsatisfied educational want, [the college] would sniff it out and attempt to satisfy it. And hence the strikingly lop-sided development.

The scene for conflict was therefore set. Entrenched departmental heads of science and technology on the one hand and a powerful and dynamic principal presiding over the arts and social sciences on the other. This division was reflected amongst the staff and indeed the disdain which those at the former college viewed those at the latter on the eve of the merger might well sum up the attitude of many a traditional technical teacher to the developments in the sixties and to the staff who benefited from them. Many saw it as 'an overnight, jumped-up college, grown too quickly, with the consequent ramshackle characteristics one would expect. Willing to run any course provided it would boost numbers, and specialising in pseudo-sciences such as sociology'.[26] As we shall see, divisions such as these set well-defined limits to the development of both a professional identity and collective consciousness amongst lecturers in public sector further and higher education and in the following decade enabled cuts in provision to go through a little more easily than might otherwise have been the case.

THE CHANGED FACE OF TECHNICAL TEACHING

Despite the difficulties involved in any summary of the diverse provision in public sector further and higher education during the years of expansion, several trends can be distinguished which significantly changed the face of technical teaching. The first and most obvious of these trends was the phenomenal growth in provision in this sector. This applied to all courses, at whatever the level and by whichever mode of attendance.

As can be seen from Table 2.1, the total number of students attending courses in the major establishments rose from some 310,000 immediately before the war to 660,000 immediately after. By 1966, the total had risen to over 1.5 million and by 1974 to almost two million students studying in the major establishments. These figures do not include those students in adult education in the evening institutes whose figures had doubled from some 900,000 to 1,800,000 during the same period.

Table 2.1: Growth in student numbers following all courses in grant-aided establishments in England and Wales 1937/8 to 1974 (in thousands)

	1938	1947	1951	1956	1961	1966	1970	1974
full-time	13.0	31.5	39.8	55.7	157.8	178.2	255.1	355.2
part-time	32.3	177.8	305.1	433.3	553.9	671.6	714.6	726.9
evening-only (major est)[a]	265.2	450.7	672.7	859.1	827.9	748.2	692.8	785.1

Notes: a. The term major establishment denotes all colleges operating under the regulations for further education other than art schools and evening institutes. Figures for 1966 onwards, therefore, do not include the CATs which came to operate under the regulations for universities at that time. The figures for 1974 onwards include colleges of art most of which had, by this time, been assimilated into the polytechnics.

Source: Board of Education Annual Report 1938/9; Ministry of Education Annual Reports 1946/7-1960; The Department of Education and Science, Statistics of Education, 1961 to present.

A second trend of note was the growing proportion of advanced to non-advanced work, with students on advanced courses comprising some 13 per cent of the total in the early sixties to some 20 per cent in the seventies, as can be seen from Table 2.2. Of particular significance here was the growth of full-time advanced-level courses which more than doubled in the decade after 1966. The increasing full-time character of these courses is important to note because the expansion in overall student numbers does not give an accurate impression of the increase in actual volume of work undertaken by the colleges during these years. A more sensitive measure of growth is the number of student hours taught rather than the number of students attending courses. For example, overall there had been a disproportionate increase in the amount of day work since the end of the war and particularly in the growth of full-time courses. The number of student hours involved in the teaching of full-time courses is considerably more than that involved in the teaching of part-time day courses which again is somewhat greater than that involved in evening-only work. Thus in the mid-fifties, whilst the number of students attending full-time day courses comprised only 4 per cent of the total number of students attending courses in the major establishments, their student hours comprised some 28 per cent of the total. Similarly, whilst the number of students attending part-time day classes was 18 per cent of the total at this time, the number of student hours involved was 41 per cent. This contrasts sharply with Richardson's statement that before the war, the technical college remained in essence a night school. However, it was not until the early seventies that full-time rather than part-time courses became the largest single contributors to the work of the colleges as measured in terms of student hours.

Table 2.2: Growth in student numbers in England and Wales by level of course and mode of study, 1951 to 1974 (nos in thousands)

	1951	1955	1961	1966	1970	1974
full-time advanced	12.4	12.2	21.4	45.7	89.7	105.7
part-time advanced	24.5	36.6	41.9	60.8	68.9	80.3
full-time non-advanced	27.4	43.4	45.5	116.8	141.0	186.6
part-time non-advanced	280.6	396.7	406.1	498.4	523.0	471.5

Source: As Table 2.1

A final trend of importance during this period was the changing content of the courses, especially at advanced level. Whilst the 1956 White Paper proposals had concentrated mainly on technical and technological education, the recommendations of the Robbins Report included higher education in all its aspects. Where the public sector was concerned, perhaps its most important recommendation was that the National Council for Technological Awards be converted into the Council for National Academic Awards (CNAA). The proposed council would have a royal charter to grant degrees (not only diplomas) for courses in all fields of study. Subject to the Council's validation procedures, the colleges could now develop their own degrees without relying, as hitherto, on the London external degree with its restricting externally imposed syllabus. The overall result of this important development was a move away from the engineering and technological subjects which had hitherto defined the technical college tradition. In 1966, for example, 52 per cent of advanced courses were in the fields of engineering and technology. By the mid-seventies this figure stood at 27 per cent, the number of actual students being 22 per cent of the total number of students following advanced courses.

This trend away from the traditional engineering and technological subjects was even more pronounced when the degrees awarded by the CNAA are examined by subject. In 1968, for example, 72 per cent of the degrees awarded were in engineering and technology, a figure which had dropped to 35 per cent by 1974. In contrast, degrees in the social science, administrative and business studies category rose from a mere 2 per cent to 26 per cent of the total during the same period. Of the total number of students reading for a degree in this category, over 50 per cent were reading general rather than applied subjects. Seventy per cent of this general group were reading sociology. A similar trend away from engineering and technology could be detected in the numbers of students following HND courses in different subjects. In engineering and technology, this number fell from 63 per cent of the total in 1966 to 48 per cent in 1974. In contrast, those following HND courses in business and commerce rose from 27 to 48 per cent of the total during the same period. National Diplomas are, of course, meant to be directly vocational in nature, but this did not mean that the growth in business studies in this area was not to the benefit of the more general social sciences. During this period, for example, a typical HND in business studies would have had economics as a compulsory subject and sociology as an option. Given such trends as these, it can be argued that during the era of expansion, the polytechnics ceased to be technical colleges in the traditional sense of the word, and became institutes of higher education offering advanced-level courses right across the academic board.

A similar trend away from engineering and technical subjects could be detected at non-advanced level but it was by no means so dramatic, total enrolments falling by some 10 per cent over the decade after 1966 to comprise 42 per cent of total enrolments by the mid-seventies. But even the continued predominance of engineering and technical subjects at non-advanced level did not mean that there were no significant developments in curriculum. From the end of the Second World War and until the change in climate in the eighties there was a growing concern that much of work-related education, being directly vocational in nature, neglected the broader educational needs of the young worker. As we have seen, such concern led to the introduction of 'liberal studies' programmes on all types of courses and taught by specially recruited arts and social science graduates.

Table 2.3: Growth and status of teachers in major establishments in England and Wales, 1938-1974

	1938	1947	1951	1956	1961	1966	1971	1974
graduate	1702	2032	3320	4944	8737	12814	18299	22396
non-graduate	1297	2489	4857	7533	13200	24190	34879	38379
total	2999	4521	8177	12477	21937	37004	53178	60775
% graduate	56.7	44.9	41.2	39.6	39.8	34.6	34.4	36.9

Source: Board of Education Annual Report 1939; Ministry of Education Annual Reports 1947-1960; Department of Education and Science, Statistics of Education, vol.4, 1966 to date.

Developments in public sector further and higher education on the scale described above could not have taken place without corresponding changes in the structure and composition of the teaching force. Again, the first and most obvious change here was in its size. Immediately before the war there were but 3,000 full-time teachers at work in the major establishments. By the end of the war this number had reached 4,521. But this was nothing compared to the explosion in numbers thereafter. As Table 2.3 indicates, the number of teachers in the major establishments almost trebled between 1947 and 1956 and in the decade following they trebled again. By the mid-seventies, the figure stood at some 61,000 representing a twenty-fold increase in the number of full-time teachers at work in the colleges over the period in question.

What is of particular interest when the composition of this massively expanded teaching force is broken down is that whilst the volume of advanced to non-advanced work increased quite considerably over these years, the proportion of graduates in the teaching force declined. This apparent contradiction indicates an important change in the structure of the profession. In further education there has always been a relatively high proportion of part-time teachers. Richardson, for example, estimated that in 1936 the 'typical' technical college had a ratio of part to full-time teachers in the order of 8 to 1.[27] Such a figure, however, obscures the enormous variation between colleges and between different departments within the same college. Taking seven different colleges, for example, Richardson showed that the overall ratio of part to full-time teachers at this time could vary from anything between 11 to 1 and 2 to 1. Within his own college, the proportions between departments varied as much as between 19 to 1 (building) and 3 to 1 (science). Indeed it was in the more directly vocational courses that the proportion of part to full-time teachers was highest and this was because the majority of such courses would have been for craft-level students who were at work during the day. So too would be their teachers who were working full-time at their trade. With the growth of day-release, however, more and more part-time teachers would have had the opportunity of becoming full-time. It would seem from Venables' survey of technical education in the mid-fifties that the overall proportion of part to full-time teachers had already dropped to something approaching 3 to 1. From the staffing details of 24 colleges (chosen to represent the contemporary range of institutions), it can be seen that the proportions varied between almost equal numbers to more than five times as many, with between twice and three times as many as the norm.[28] By 1970, Cantor and Roberts put the limits at between twice and one half the number of full-time members of staff.[29]

The increase in full and part-time day work together with the increasing rationalisation of the colleges in the years following the 1956 White Paper resulted in another significant change in the structure of the occupation. From the small, scattered profession of pre-war years, it became more 'mass-like' in character with much larger numbers of staff concentrated in fewer establishments. No longer were there colleges where the principal might have no full-time members of staff working under him as in the mid-twenties, nor where a head of department might be responsible for between only three and six full-time members of staff as in the mid-fifties. By the mid-thirties, the colleges employed many more full-time members of staff, though still considerably less than after the era of expansion was complete. In Venables' sample of 24 colleges, for example, nine employed less than 50 full-time members of staff; twelve between 50 and 100 and only three between 100 and 200.[30] In contrast, in the writer's own survey of 41 colleges in the West Midlands in the seventies, only six colleges had under 50 full-time members of staff and a further ten had between 50 and 100. The bulk of the colleges had between 100 and 200 members with a further four standing at between 250 and 400. The two largest colleges in the area had over 500 full-time lecturers in post.

However, the trend towards concentration was to a certain extent offset by increasing differentiation within the profession. Since the war, there has been a proliferation of teaching grades along hierarchical lines and defined with increasing rigidity according to level of work taught rather than teaching ability, qualifications and experience. Thus whilst before the war there were but two teaching grades below that of head of department, by 1956 there were four, and by the sixties no less than 5 (excluding the post of reader which is primarily a research post and applies only to the polytechnics in any great number). It can be seen from Table 2.4 that the number of teachers in what are strictly teaching grades (principal lecturer and below) increased significantly relative to the administrative or managerial posts which fell from 20 per cent of the total in 1938 to a mere 6 per cent in recent years. As we shall see, the proliferation of teaching posts was a force for considerable disunity within the profession and at least in part response to this the trend was reversed after the mid-seventies with the abolition of the assistant lecturer grade and an increasing element of automatic progression through the salary scales.

Table 2.4: Grades of teaching staff in post 1938 to 1974

	No.	%		No.	%
1938			**1956**		
Principal	265	9	Principal	440	4
Head of Department	342	11	Vice-Principal	107	1
Assistant	2100	70	Head of Department	937	8
Instructor	291	10	Senior Lecturer	724	6
			Lecturer	2211	18
			Assistant Grade B	4315	35
			Assistant Grade A	3382	28
1966			**1974**		
Principal	620	2	Principal	588	1
Vice-Principal	302	1	Vice-Principal	494	1
Head of Department	1872	5	Head of Department	2557	4
Principal Lecturer	519	1	Principal Lecturer	2631	4
Senior Lecturer	3402	9	Senior Lecturer	9412	16
Lecturer	9126	25	Lecturer Grade II	20121	34
Assistant Grade B	16661	45	Lecturer Grade I	21390	35
Assistant Grade A	4284	12	Assistant Lecturer	2997	5

Source: Board of Education Annual Report 1938; Ministry of Education Annual Report 1956; Statistics of Education, vol.4, 1960 to date.

The Era of Expansion

Given the changes in curriculum during the years of expansion, it was not surprising that by the end of that era the composition of the teaching force had also changed significantly. The proportion of technology graduates fell from 24 per cent of the total in 1956 to 14 per cent by 1974. There was a decline of the same magnitude in the proportion of mathematics and science graduates. In contrast the number of social science graduates rose to 27.5 per cent of the total during the same period. In this regard, it is also interesting to note that certain groups of teachers differed significantly in their age distribution from others. Graduates, for example, tended to be younger than non-graduates. This reflected the different backgrounds of the two groups. Graduates would enter teaching soon after graduating whilst non-graduates spent some time in industry working at the trade or profession they come to teach. Many will have gained their qualifications whilst working. Similarly, technology graduates were older as a group than other graduates for they too were likely to have spent some time in industry, either through choice or necessarily to become fully qualified members of their respective professional associations. This helps to explain why the age distribution within the profession remained remarkably constant during the period in question, despite its enormous growth and the high number of new recruits each year. In 1956, for example, 12 per cent of college lecturers were under thirty and a further 36 per cent were under forty. By the mid-seventies, the number of teachers under thirty had risen to only 15 per cent and those between thirty and forty had actually declined. By contrast at this point some 38 per cent of schoolteachers were under the age of thirty and a further 22 per cent under the age of forty. As the era of expansion came to an end, the college lecturers began to look even older as a group compared with the school-teachers, with only 5 per cent of their number being under thirty at the beginning of the eighties.

One final point about the composition of the teaching force in public sector further and higher education worth noting was the small proportion of women within the profession. This was almost negligible in pre-war years when science and technology predominated and the teachers of domestic science were organised in their own association. Despite the rapid increase in the arts and social science subjects during the era of expansion, women still comprised only 16 per cent of the teaching force in the early seventies, a figure which rose to a little over 20 per cent in the early eighties given the amalgamation of many teacher training colleges with the polytechnics and other major establishments. In contrast something in excess of 60 per cent of schoolteachers are women.

NOTES

1. T. Burgess & J. Pratt, Policy and Practice, The Colleges of Advanced Technology (Allen Lane, 1972), p.19.
2. Higher Technological Education, (Percy Report, 1945). For a useful summary of these and other recommendations embodied in the report see M. Argles, South Kensington to Robbins (Longmans, 1964).
3. Burgess and Pratt, Policy and Practice, p.22.
4. See, for example, Education in 1949, Ministry of Education Annual Report. Unless otherwise stated, all statistics in this chapter derive from the official statistics for the relevant year.
5. Education in 1954, (Ministry of Education), p.22. The criteria for approval for such courses was rigorous and had a significant effect on raising the standards and improving the conditions of service in the aspiring colleges. Amongst them were that there should be a high standard of accommodation and equipment, suitable facilities for both adequate teaching and research in technology and the natural sciences and well-qualified staff with considerable freedom in planning courses. In addition future policies were anticipated in the Ministry's insistence on a good proportion of advanced work already existing in the colleges.
6. Quoted in S. Cotgrove, Technical Education and Social Change (Allen & Unwin, 1958), p.171. See ibid. pp.167-85 and Burgess and Pratt, Policy and Practice, pp.19-28, for a more detailed analysis of the different interests involved in the debate.
7. Eric Robinson, The New Polytechnics (Penguin, 1968), p.22.
8. Burgess and Pratt, Policy and Practice, p.24.
9. Ibid.
10. Quoted in Cotgrove, Technical Education and Social Change, p.178.
11. Ibid. The ATTI was itself conscious that the reluctance of the universities to expand in the field of applied science was at least in part responsible for their good fortune. One article, 'A Century of British Education'

in the Technical Journal in June 1951, for example, argues quite forcibly that 'had some of the universities come earlier to believe that their function included research and teaching not only in science but in applied science also, and they had therefore forged closer links with industry ... the technical colleges might have been able to confine themselves to the education of craftsmen and technicians'.

12. Burgess & Pratt, Policy and Practice, p.40.

13. Beryl Tipton, Conflict and Change in a Technical College (Hutchinson, 1973).

14. See Anthony Crosland's speeches at Woolwich, 1965, where he first outlined the binary policy and at Lancaster University, 1967, where he defended it against attack. It has been suggested by both the ATTI and others that the policy was inspired by the ATTI policy statement, 'The Future of Higher Education within the Further Education System', which sought an expansion in advanced work in as many public sector colleges as possible. The ATTI, however, whilst at first welcoming the policy as a recognition of the technical college tradition, soon came to condemn it in its drive to rationalise and create what the ATTI thought might be yet another set of elite institutions divorced from the rest of further education.

15. The Carr Report, Training for Skills, had in 1958 proposed a significant extension of day release but had at the same time recommended that the State should continue to leave industrial training to the voluntary efforts of employers.

16. For a detailed outline of the sort of changes made in the structure of courses and the machinery for their development and implementation consequent upon the White Paper see Leonard M. Cantor & I.F. Roberts, Further Education in England and Wales (RKP, 1972) and D.F. Bratchell, The Aims and Organisation of Further Education (Pergamon, 1968). Bratchell also gives interesting details of the high degree of wastage on part-time evening courses during this period.

17. The Crowther Report, 15 to 18, 1959. For a useful summary of the report see Bratchell, Aims and Organisation, pp.14-20.

18. 'Industrial Training and Further Education - A Further Statement', Central Training Council, Memo. no. 4, 1966.

19. Cited in Cantor and Roberts, Further Education, p.89.

20. Ethel Venables, The Young Worker at College (Faber, 1967).

21. Beryl Tipton, Conflict and Change, p.95.

22. E. Venables, The Young Worker, p.130.

23. Ibid. p.131.

24. Statistics of Education, vol.4, 1974.

25. C. Cox et al., 'Notes on The Polytechnic of North London', unpublished paper, 1973.

26. Ibid.

27. W.A. Richardson, The Technical College, Its Organisation and Administration (Oxford University Press, 1939), p.134.

28. Peter Venables, Technical Education, Its Aims, Organisation and Future Development (Bell, 1956).

29. Cantor and Roberts, Further Education, p.182.

30. P. Venables, Technical Education, Its Aims and Organisation.

PART TWO

THE GROWTH OF A TRADE UNION

3
Professional Association

PROFESSIONALISM AS AN IDEOLOGY
The aims of The Association of Teachers in Technical Institutions as issued in a circular proposing an inaugural meeting of London technical teachers in 1904 were set out as follows:

1. The advancement of technical education generally.

2. The interchange regarding methods of technical teaching.

3. The promotion and safeguarding of the professional interests of technical teachers in such matters as tenure, pensions, salaries, registration of teachers, and schemes of examination and inspection.

4. To lay the views of technical teachers before various educational bodies and the public.

5. To enable technical teachers to co-operate as a body with other educational and scientific bodies where desirable.[1]

It is no coincidence that the advancement of technical education should find priority on this list. During these early years a cursory glance at the pages of the Technical Journal (the official journal of the Association) well illustrates their pre-occupation with educational issues. Indeed, it was precisely this concern with expertise and knowledge which led many early (and some not so early) social theorists to under-emphasise the essential protective function of such associations, elevating instead self-proclaimed notions of service to the community and disavowal of self-interest to their defining characteristic. Evidence suggests, however, that the impetus to association amongst technical teachers, as indeed amongst other groups of professionals, was intimately bound up with their occupational self-interest. That the impetus to association amongst technical as well as other teachers was the necessity for representation on educational matters should not be surprising from this point of view. As J.J. Graves, first president of the National Union of Teachers said in his inaugural address, 'there is no class of men whose daily duties and personal interests are more frequently interfered with by legislation and hence teachers must of necessity unite and influence such legislation'.[2]

That concern over educational issues was integral to their protective function is evidenced by the lines along which the educational policy of the teachers' associations were drawn. Indeed, so much was education policy determined by the sectional interests of the teachers concerned that at least one contemporary social reformer was forced to throw up her hands in despair:

> Do not associations of teachers sit at the same time in the same town and pass contradictory or incompatible resolutions ... such that the organisation which purports to represent the profession finds its influence on the ratepayers' representatives and on the Board of Education correspondingly diminished.[3]

The ATTI was no exception and it is impossible to understand either its pre-occupation with educational matters during these early years, or the content of its education policy, without reference to two basic facts; the marginal status of technical education in the education system as a whole and the unity of interest which technical teachers saw between the advancement of technical education and their own advancement. As they saw it, to increase the status of the technical teacher, it was necessary first to increase the status of technical education. The logic was simple, if largely mistaken.[4] Once the status of technical education had been raised so too must be the status of the technical teacher. The status of the technical teacher secured, so must there follow the commensurate material rewards. It was based on observation of the high status professions, the lawyers, doctors and the traditional secondary school teacher. Was not the status of their occupations high and their level of remuneration commensurate?

Thus it was that a great deal of time was spent on the

advancement of technical education. This generally took the form of proclaiming its central importance to a successful industrial nation. As one president of the Association put it during the backlash against technical education in the early years of the century:

> It is our duty to keep always in the foreground of public attention the dependence of industrial progress upon scientific and technical education. The need for our activities as advocates of technical education is all the greater at the present time, when there is a chance of public attention being engrossed by the demands of elementary and secondary education at the expense of technical education.[5]

The technical teachers wanted to see an integrated system of technologically-oriented education from the primary right through to the post-graduate stage, with the technological universities lending prestige to the day technical schools as Oxbridge lent prestige to the traditional secondary school. Conscious of developments subsequent to the 1902 Secondary Education Act when technical subjects had been squeezed out by the more traditional academic subjects, the secondary school which was to feed the technological university was to be separate but equal. Indeed, so determined were they not to see such a repetition of events that they were the only teachers' association after the First World War actively to oppose the movement towards 'secondary education for all' on the grounds that the secondary education which was being proposed would be too literary in character. 'Youths', they thought, 'would continue to be pitchforked into pursuits for which they are not adapted or into professions which are overcrowded.'[6]

They pressed instead for continuation schools which were to be an alternative to the traditional secondary schools, the purveyors of a totally new type of culture and one more suitable to an industrial age. It was crucial that such schools, whilst different, should be equal in status. Their idea of a continuation school, for example, was not that which was proposed by Fisher in his Education Bill of 1918. Fisher's schools, they felt, would approximate more closely to the elementary schools and training would not be materially better than that which then obtained for the elementary teachers. The schools proposed by the technical teachers, on the other hand, would be 'institutions which in matters of corporate life, breadth of education, esprit de corps, influence on character and even curriculum would be somewhat analogous to the secondary schools with, in appropriate centres, a special bias towards technical education in the last two years'. Obviously, such a high status technical school would have implications for the status of the technical teacher: 'the teachers,' they argued, 'consequently should have a status and possess qualifications comparable with those in the secondary schools.'[7]

In fact what the technical teachers were trying to do was to re-create the old Higher Grade Schools on a firmer basis and under their own control, not under that of the more academically-minded secondary school teachers. For some time during these early years it had seemed that this might be achieved with the development of the junior technical schools which had grown up on the basis of a clause in the 1905 Board of Education Regulations giving aid to technical institutes for day technical classes designed to meet the needs of pupils who had completed their elementary education. Whilst at first the technical teachers had gladly accepted the official restriction that such schools should meet the needs of future artisans (recruitment being at the age of 13 when the brightest of children had already passed into the secondary schools) and definitely not for the preparation of pupils training for the higher positions in industries who stay at school or technical institutes until the age of seventeen or eighteen, they were not long content with this once the position of the schools was assured. By 1914 they were protesting strongly against any attempts to make of such schools an avenue to artisan status only and agitation to lower the age of entry began in earnest. To the eventual suggestion by the Board of Education that local authorities wishing to reorganise their technical schools to recruit at the age of eleven should experiment instead with secondary schools with a moderate commercial or industrial bias, they were singularly unreceptive, criticising that attitude of mind which 'involved a vague conviction that a liberal education is inherent in the humanities' and 'tends to receive technical education in a somewhat cold and superior fashion'. The work of the technical schools, they claimed had taken away from the word technical 'that atmosphere suggestive of nothing more than the art of earning a living, and have made it indicate the art of living itself'. 'The Junior Technical Schools,' they continued, 'should be regarded not merely as providing an education to fit pupils for the modern world as we know it, but as formulating a new type of education calculated to produce a new culture to replace ultimately the older values which seem now so obviously crumbling.[8]

The pages of the Technical Journal were full of such powerful ideas as to what technical education could and should be, powerful ideas which, as we have seen, bore little resemblance to reality during these early years. The Association's policy towards secondary education after the First World War was attacked as both self-interested and reactionary by the supporters of the 'secondary education for all' movement. Never in these early years were the demands of the technical teachers in the mainstream of educational thought and unlike the elementary school teachers, they could not rely on the Labour Movement for support. Discussing the reaction to his own Education Bill in 1918, Fisher himself remarked on 'the suspicion of all forms of vocational training which was then so prevalent among official exponents of Labour Philosophy'.[9] That the technical teachers themselves were well aware of their lack of friends is clear not only from their grandiose attempts to redefine the whole concept of technical education, but also from their continual laments on popular definitions of technical education as mere vocational training. As one editorial in the Technical Journal pointedly remarked:

> Technical teachers have always had a very difficult role to play in the educational world, being suspected on the one hand by organised workers as being the instrument for the training of better profit-earning machines and on the other hand furtively (sometimes openly) sneered at by the high-brow academicians as 'the purveyors of soiled goods'.[10]

However, attempts to change popular definitions of the potentiality of technical education were, to say the least, a long-term goal and in the immediate it was to the development of higher technological education that technical teachers looked for their salvation. Technical teachers, it seems, were even at this time trying to capture higher-level, full-time work at the expense of lower-level, part-time courses. Millis, Principal of Borough Polytechnic, was much dismayed by the tendency of the larger technical institutes to concentrate on high-level day work. He argued passionately that such courses were not designed:

> For the type of persons for whom, under the Charity Commissioners' Schemes, they were established. The best students of the type who ought to attend Polytechnics, who show ability for higher work could be passed by scholarship to institutions which specialise in such education. The preparation of students for degrees of the University of London is no doubt an excellent object ... but if Technical Institutes take up this work there is a danger of their becoming sham University Colleges instead of places of education for workers either about to be or already engaged in industrial occupations.[11]

That many technical teachers would have violently disagreed with such an educational philosophy is apparent in the indignation shown over the proposals put forward by the Royal Commission on University Education in 1910 which would have effectively stripped the technical institutes of high-level work and research. The root of the Commission's objections to high-level work in the institutes was not the same as that of Millis, whose sole concern was that more practical education for the working class should not suffer. Rather, the Commission's objections were rooted in the old class ideas as to the 'natural' institutions for the training of different ranks of society. 'The Universities,' argued Blair, Education Officer for the London County Council, in his evidence to the Committeee, 'are for making officers: the Polytechnics were intended to make the rank and file the most capable rank and file in the world.'[12] The existence of high and low-level work side by side, countered the technical teachers, had the effect of raising the general quality of work and improved the status and efficiency of the staffs. To the old argument of the right kind of 'atmosphere' in the universities, the technical teachers countered the 'spirit' of the polytechnics and denied vehemently that their staffs were in the main any less qualified for recognition by London University than any other university teachers. To maintain this high calibre, however, it was important that any technological research funds should come the way of the technical institutes. 'Research,' the <u>Technical Journal</u> tells us in 1915, 'may be the agent for raising the status of the teacher, so giving him a long-cherished desire.'

Emphasising the essentially protective function of the technical teachers' concern with educational issues is not meant to deny that they were passionately convinced of the importance of technical education. On the contrary, the leadership at very least were dedictated fighters for technical education both for itself as well as for the interests of the teachers. On issues directly affecting the quality of technical education, the leadership continually took a firm stand. On the question of examinations, for example, they were adamant that external control should be relaxed, advocating instead a system of 'grouped' courses to be developed by the teachers themselves in close contact with industry. From the very beginnings of the Association, subject groups had been set up whose job it was to draw up complete systems of education for each trade or profession which their members were engaged in teaching and the reports of their meetings formed the bulk of material published in the early Technical Journal. Even their concern with salaries might be considered more purely altruistic given the undeniable relationship which exists between the salaries of teachers and the quality of staff recruited to the profession. It did indeed seem that the leadership of the Association was often irritated by what it considered to be the technical teacher's over-concern with more narrowly trade union issues. For example, in response to a remark made by a non-member to the effect that the Association was not better supported because technical teachers 'were too well-off and had but few grievances to redress', came the retort:

> Are we thoroughly clear as to the true meaning of our principle aim ... 'the advancement of technical education'? It is common experience to hear individual members speak of the Association as if its principal objects were to obtain legal advice gratis, a rise in salaries or a superannuation fund - all most praiseworthy doubtless but hardly of sufficient high moral standard to justify our existence.[13]

'The question we should ask ourselves,' said one Principal high-ranking in the Association, 'is not so much how the Association is going to benefit us, but how it is going to benefit education.'[14]

The aim here is not to deny the more purely education function of such associations, but to assert the intricate relationship which existed between education policy and self-interest, for unless we understand that their fundamental nature as organisational forms was to protect the interests of their members, we shall understand neither their early character nor their subsequent development into more trade union-like bodies. It was not the ATTI's concern with education in these early years which made it unlike a trade union in character, but the ways in which the Association saw its members' interests being achieved. By defining the more narrowly professional problems such as salaries and conditions of service as essentially a matter of their low social standing and in seeing the problem to be remedied by raising the status of technical education, the technical teachers were following a strategy which whilst having fundamentally the same goals as the trade unions, had little in common with the strategies they employed.

Indeed, the basis of the ATTI's strategy might be broken down into two component parts consisting of what Elliott, for example, has called 'status professionalism' on the one hand and 'occupational professionalism' on the other.[15] Status professionalism owes its origins to that historical point in time when the position of the professions in society depended not on the market value of a specialised body of knowledge or expertise, but on their relationship to high-status groups in society. The necessary qualification to be a member of a profession was that of being a gentleman. Thus, to be a professional was more a symbol of social status than a job specification. It stressed the independence of the professional from the employer and even from work itself. As Marshall put it, 'the professional man does not work in order to be paid, he is paid in order that he may work'.[16] The professional, then, was not concerned with the base self-interested pursuit of profit and, above all, a distance was kept from trade or commerce.

By the end of the nineteenth century, however, social and economic changes had combined to create whole new sections of society who, whilst not common labourers, had not the means to live without earning a living. At the same time an increasingly complex division of labour opened up new opportunities for them to do so. Here we see the origins of that process whereby occupation acquired its significance as a key indicator of social status. This development gave rise to 'occupational professionalism', or the creation of opportunities to meet specialised demand and the assertion of knowledge and skill in support of claims for economic security and social standing. Such was the historical point in time that technical teaching as a profession was born. The emphasis which the technical teachers placed on the importance of technical education and the expertise which was necessary to perform the job might usefully be interpreted within the strategy of 'occupational professionalism' which, as such, need not necessarily have been in contradiction to trade unionism. Ideologically, however, they were trapped within the confines of 'status professionalism', the ideals of public service rather than personal gain, the attributes of the 'professional gentleman' to whose position in society they aspired. Status for the technical teacher was thus both a strategy and a tactic. Social status with its material rewards was their goal, establishing the status and respectability of their occupation the means of achieving it. In the prevailing social climate, this precluded any approximation to the trade-union model whatsoever.

TRADE UNION ISSUES
Thus the technical teachers' approach to more narrowly defined trade-union issues during these early years was informed by both the strategy of occupational professionalism and the values of status professionalism. They continued to re-assert the importance of technical education and the expertise necessary to do the job of technical teaching. At the same time, their concern over such issues as salaries and conditions of service was rarely voiced without reference to the good of technical education and the consequent well-being of the country. Without adequate remuneration, the argument would go, the technical teachers would be unable to render the service which their sense of vocation demanded. That service was of vital importance if the country was to succeed and prosper as an industrial nation. Thus it was that after years of inflation, when the technical teachers had suffered disproportionately in relation to both other teachers and to other sections of the community, their claims for more money continued to be presented in altruistic terms. 'The technical teacher,' we were told in 1917, 'must be properly appreciated by the nation if his work is to have the success the country requires. His status must be raised if he is to give the best

67

of which he is capable. We must tell the world that we cannot do the task before us unless our conditions of work are good. No man can work strenuously and unselfishly if he has not a modicum of the goods things in life.'

Such proclamations were not merely a calculated presentation of self for public consumption. Rather, they overcame the very real contradiction between the growing need to be concerned with salaries in and of themselves and their self-image as professional gentlefolk concerned to serve irrespective of self-interest. This contradiction was common amongst the teachers of the day and the manner of its resolution is perhaps best summed up in the words of the President of the Association of Assistant Mistresses writing in 1907:

> Early in its history the Association realised how powerfully the status of the teacher reacts upon her work; and it took a sympathetic part in the pioneer investigations made in 1887 ... with regard to salaries. At first this action gave rise to heart-quakings and even misconception on the part of some of our members. Many, fearing that the A.A.M. savoured too strongly of Trade Unionism, hastily withdrew their membership. It is often the names of things rather than the realities which terrify ... It is not too much to say that from all class-unionism, which means the banding together of individuals inspired by a common selfish aim - that of grasping power or profit with little thought of service - the Association has ever kept itself free. If, however, Trade Unionism can mean the banding together of individuals recognising their common interest in order to obtain such conditions of labour as shall react favourably on the work itself, then we may plead guilty to Trade Unionism.

During these early years, she continued, those 'less concerned with the quality of their service' or who were merely less 'far-sighted', 'were loth to do anything so vulgar as to press their claims to more adequate salaries'.[17]

Thus trade unionism in the normal sense of the word was almost a term of abuse for these professional employees, not because it was an inappropriate model of organisation as such, but because they were ideologically opposed to its principles. This becomes clearer if we look at the manner in which claims to more adequate remuneration were pursued. Where salaries were concerned, the Association's first step was to draw up the average of salaries as they already existed in the profession both as a guide to the local authorities and to strengthen the hand of the individual teacher in negotiation with an authority where pay was poor. It soon became painfully obvious, however, that salaries as they existed were inadequate and the Association's tactics changed from merely providing information to drawing up appropriate salary scales to be pressed collectively on the local authorities. Early salary policy centred around parity with the secondary school teachers. In 1911, for example, the starting salary for the secondary school teacher was £150 whilst the average for the technical teacher was £151. In 1914, average salaries stood at £175 and £165 respectively. Eighty per cent of technical teachers were in receipt of less than £251 per annum, the baseline for inclusion in the provisions of the Liberal Party's Insurance Act of 1906.[18] Indeed, such was the outcry at this prospect that the secondary, technical and university teachers, failing to convince the government of the need for a state-financed scheme especially for them, set up their own superannuation scheme, STUTIS (Secondary, Technical and University Teachers' Insurance Scheme) based, as one correspondent to the Technical Journal noted approvingly, 'on the principle of self-help'. The outcry was in part concerned with practical difficulties, but there was a large element of outrage at being included in an Act designed principally for 'mere' workmen. The technical teachers' case for a state-aided pension scheme had been argued in terms of the dignity it would lend the profession, and dignity was certainly not to be conferred by a labourer's insurance card.

In pressing salary claims on the local authorities, great emphasis was placed on the power of the reasoned case and the justice of the teachers' claim. No conflict of interest between the teachers and their employers was hinted at, disagreements being explained in terms of a 'misunderstanding' of the teachers' position. Great emphasis was placed on 'educating' the education committees. At Bradford, for example, where a lecturer's post had been advertised at £60 per annum, the Association was convinced that 'on reflection the authorities must see that such salaries must ultimately exert a detrimental influence on the progress of technical education'.[19] The strategy of educating the authorities as to the importance of technical education had important implications for tactics. Great stress was put on numbers in the Association, not as with a trade union, to increase bargaining power, but to increase its credibility as the representative voice of professional opinion. Furthermore, if the local authorities were to be persuaded to listen, it followed that the ATTI's most responsible and illustrious members should do the talking; hence it was that both the Council and the Executive Committee during these early years were dominated by principals and heads of department. Stress on the need to influence the powers-that-be also necessitated unimpeachable professional conduct. In a recruiting leaflet of 1908, for example, it was stressed that the Association had gained a recognised place in the educational world 'by its careful and prudent actions'. The one half-session at Conference devoted to trade union issues was held in private, no mention of its deliberations being reported in even the Technical Journal. In public pronouncements care was continually taken to distance themselves from the trade union movement. Indeed, in his inaugural address in 1907, the Association's first president saw fit to spend some time on the issue of trade unionism:

> The authorities view our Association with favour, though they are a little on their guard lest we should become a technical teachers' trade union ... They need have no fear, I think, as if such an unfortunate event should come about there would inevitably be a breaking up of the Association, a catastrophy we should all deplore ... Local Authorities will, I am sure, be always ready to listen to what teachers have to say, and their views, moderately expressed, must always have an enlightening influence.[20]

It was not always the case, however, that the authorities chose to be enlightened. In 1907, for example, West Ham Council decided to lower the existing scales for teachers and the NUT was forced into action, holding first public meetings and conferences in the Borough, then withdrawing teachers from the schools and threatening mass resignations. The actions of Herefordshire County Council in 1910 were a similar case in point. They positively refused to implement any salary scales for teachers and this time the

NUT resorted to strikes on such a large scale that more than sixty schools in the area were closed down.

Although in both cases the actions of the local authorities would have seriously affected the technical teachers, there was no explicit reference to either dispute in the <u>Technical Journal</u>. The least which this silence might tell us would be that the <u>Technical Journal</u> was no campaigning journal in these early years, in keeping with the Association's image as a body concerned primarily with the advancement of technical education and which relied on 'cautious statesmanship' to achieve its ends. It takes on more definite meaning, however, if we consider the Association's reactions to subsequent events in the educational world. For example, it is ironic that during the First World War, throughout which the importance of technical education came increasingly to be recognised, the technical teachers were the only section of the teaching profession not to get a supplementary grant to lessen the effects of war-time inflation. Whilst it is true that 'for patriotic reasons' the technical teachers had never actually demanded a war bonus (as had, for example, the NUT), they had certainly hinted strongly that 'help was needed'. The strength of their reaction would indicate that they had expected better treatment:

> Have we passed away from the old time of 100 years ago when the indigent and useless, the cripple, the broken sailor, the clerical failure might buy a candle and open a night school receiving payment in kind - a few pots, a turf of brick or in coppers ... Is the technical teacher this poor thing - a remedy for the misfits turned out from the elementary and the secondary schools. Or is the work of the technical teacher above and beyond the work that these lower schools can do? Why then has the President of the Board of Education made a distinction between the secondary and elementary teachers on the one hand and the technical teachers on the other?[21]

The answer to this question could not be formulated in terms of the lack of importance accorded to technical education, indeed Fisher had given it his blessing in his Education Bill. Rather, the answer lay outside the ideological confines of the Association. The supplementary grants had been given to the other teachers because of the agitation of the NUT, which, in 1916 had entered into negotiations with the authorities for higher salaries and had threatened strike action when they broke down. Faced with an imminent breakdown of the education service due to both the war-time shortage of teachers and the activities of the NUT, the government was forced to make extra money available. But rather than satisfy the elementary teachers, the bonus seemed to whet their appetite, and the immediate post-war years saw strikes in no less than 32 different areas. It is without doubt this deep unrest amongst the elementary teachers which secured the setting up of the Burnham Committees in 1919, the first national joint negotiating machinery for teachers, whose explicit aim was to bring about an 'orderly and progressive solution to the salary problem'. Even after the institution of Burnham, the NUT faced some of the bitterest strikes in its history to secure the implementation of the agreed scales by recalcitrant local authorities. As a result, the implementation of the Burnham awards was made compulsory on local authorities in 1926.

The technical teachers, however, declined to learn from this experience. On the contrary, even when criticising the treatment meted out to them during the war years, they were more concerned than ever to emphasise the responsible character of their Association. At their conference in 1920, for example, the President made a thinly-veiled and well-received attack on the militancy of the school teachers:

> Technical teaching and technical teachers must not be made the strap-hangers of education, not treated as an unwanted child ... The advances that have come the way of other teachers have not yet reached the technical teachers ... I am glad to say, however, that the technical teachers have loyally stuck to their work (Applause) ... They are convinced of the justice of their claims and are confident that they will be met. Their only cry is 'let it be soon'.[22]

During a period of heightened trade union militancy from which many white-collar unions were not exempt, the Association made not the slightest move towards more trade-union oriented behaviour. At their conference in Wales in 1921, one unfortunate after-dinner speaker under some illusion as to the character of the ATTI, welcomed the guests with remarks to the effect that he had always been in favour of trade unionism and how nice it was to see trade unionism amongst groups of workers hitherto unorganised. The response of the then president, a Professor G. Knox, himself an ex-miner, was both forceful and uncomprising: 'The ATTI is not a trade union,' he replied, 'does not agree with the normal trade union methods and certainly would never go out on strike.'[23]

Nowhere was this difference in strategy and tactics more apparent than in the ATTI's understanding of the setting up of the Burnham Committees. The NUT was convinced that Burnham was a response to their resolute salary fights. One leader of the NUT wrote in 1931 that Fisher, President of the Board of Education responsible for Burnham, 'saw clearly enough that an underpaid, restless, resentful teaching profession was a menace to the state', and 'knew that teachers possessed a power in the community that would make itself felt'.[24] According to the School-master at the time, Fisher was not the only politician to realise the significance of the European revolutions of 1917 when at the head of every continental revolutionary movement, or near the head of it, there stood an ex-teacher. The ATTI, on the other hand, saw the setting up of the Burnham Committees rather differently. 'Burnham Committees', they claimed, 'are a very satisfactory recognition of the Associations and of their sense of responsibility and self-government.' In reply to the NUT's bitter struggles to gain the implementation of the awards, the ATTI stated that Burnham was nothing more nor less than a 'gentlemen's agreement', the provisions of which were not to be made into 'tools of aggression on the part of the teachers'.[25]

THE ATTI AND THE NUT

Given that both the ATTI and the NUT were faced with very similar problems during these early years, the question presents itself as to why they were so different in character. Despite a similarity in the social background of their membership and a common concern over social status, the NUT showed a readiness to respond to problems in a trade union-like manner which was conspicuous in its absence from the ATTI. Structural factors in each profession were at least in part responsible. To begin with, it is important to note that throughout much of the early history of the NUT, its leadership was little different in orientation from that of the ATTI. Professional gentlemen by instinct, they too were careful to point out that their association was no trade union in the normal sense of the word. Under the leadership of T.E. Heller, General Secretary of the Union from 1873 to 1891, it concentrated on such activities as sending deputations to Parliament and local education committees as well as building up a strong legal department to deal with individual 'cases of oppression'. As with the ATTI, the leadership of the Union during this period rested in the hands of the most prominent members of the profession: they were almost without exception head teachers.

Then the structure of the profession began to change. Beatrice Webb, for example, argues that by the turn of the century:

> The multiplication of schools slackened and those in the densely populated centres grew in size, so that a single head teacher found himself in command of a dozen or even a score of class teachers. It became apparent that a majority of assistants would remain in that position throughout their working lives.[26]

Blocked mobility combined with the head teachers' carelessness of the more pressing material needs of their assistants to produce a powerful organisation of class teachers within the NUT, an organisation which, Tropp tells us, 'besides their particular grievances of salary and promotion, tended to be more militant, left-wing and trade-union minded'.[27] And it was these class teachers who during the years of crisis 'would manage either to capture leadership positions for themselves or pressurise the existing leadership into taking action'.[28] It is significant, for example, that at the beginning of the war, the NUT leadership had called off its already existing salary campaign for fear it would be considered 'unpatriotic and selfish'. As it became apparent that far from general want, wage rates were rising, overtime was the rule and war bonuses were conceded on demand, the Executive were faced with an increasingly restive rank and file. First it wavered, then it re-opened the salary claim to threats of strike action from annual conference.

In comparison, there was no organised opposition to the

leadership within the ATTI. The composition of the Executive Committee changed little during these years and the officers of the Association were chosen from amongst this already select few. As one ex-president of the Association from these early years put it in correspondence with the writer:

> There is no doubt but that many of the influential members of the ATTI were of the Old Guard brigade, e.g. Heads of Colleges or Heads of Department chiefly from the larger cities or towns ... Possibly policy adopted by the Heads might not be in the interests of the underlings whom they controlled: as far as unionism was concerned - whether it be the NUT or the TUC, it was anathema to them. But really this question in my time (pre-1930) was hardly discussed at all.[29]

There is no doubt, however, that by the 1920s there was dissatisfaction amongst the 'underlings' in the ATTI. 1921 saw a revolt of rate-payers against educational expenditure with deputations of tradesmen going to Parliament to demand cuts. The government advised the teachers to decline to take up the salary increment due to them, forgo £5,000,000 of their salary grant and pay a 5 per cent contribution to the cost of their pensions (the teachers had won a non-contributory scheme in 1919). Whilst the teachers refused to comply with any of these suggestions, the government was supported by the Geddes Committee on Public Expenditure which reported in February, 1922. In May that year, legislation was passed to the effect that teachers should pay 5 per cent of their salaries to the superannuation scheme. Later that same year, the teachers were asked, through the Burnham Committees, to offer a 'voluntary' reduction of 5 per cent of their salaries for the following financial year. They consented for fear of the more drastic reductions the government threatened to impose should they fail to agree. For much of the same reason they offered a further 'abatement' the following year and were much disappointed when an arbitration committee proposed in addition a 'halt' such that the first increment in salary occurred after two years not one, with consequential effect upon all teachers' salaries.

The fact that the abatements were 'voluntary' was described in terms indicating something of a minor victory by the leadership of the ATTI. There were hints, however, of some dissension. The Executive Committee's resolution to accept the first abatement was passed through Council by only a small majority and as the abatements continued the Technical Journal saw for the first time in its history reports from branches which were at odds with official policy. Some urged the adoption of a more fighting policy and one correspondent went as far as to question the time-honoured priorities of the leadership, challenging them to look at the different levels of attendance at branch meetings concerned with, for example, the proposed salary cuts or the ethics of technical education. He argued that the membership were far more concerned with bread and butter issues than the leadership cared to admit. As might be expected, these same years produced attempts both to limit the power of the Executive and to influence its composition. West Ham, for example, wanted to see a postal ballot on all matters of importance affecting the whole Association and Leicestershire wanted to ensure that out of the ten representatives on the Burnham Committee not more than one would be a principal.

Such dissatisfaction as there was remained ineffective, but this does not necessarily mean that it was mere token protest. As such, any disaffected, potentially militant member would have found it very difficult to organise effective opposition to the 'Old Guard' given both the structure of the occupation and the small numbers in the Association. It must be remembered that the militant class teacher in the NUT might find himself active in a local association of 600 or more members. The NUT itself was at this time some 100,000 strong. This, together with the fact that the average elementary teacher had little chance of mobility, either within the profession or into occupations outside, provided a field ripe for organisation. The situation of the technical teacher could not have been more different. The local branch was small and branches were spread thinly over large geographical areas. So diverse was their occupational background and training that the Association could justly claim that 'no Association of teachers at all approaches that of the technical teachers in the heterogeneous character of its members and hence the diverse nature of their qualifications'.[30] Not only did technical teachers have little common experience or training which might bind them together, there is evidence to suggest that status distinctions between, for example, the craft teacher and the graduate, actually kept them apart. In additon, there existed in the larger technical institutes which might have allowed for some unity of action a competition for resources unlike anything which was known in the world of the school teacher.

For example, the technical institutes were divided into small departments each depending for its existence on its ability to attract students whose attendance was purely voluntary. This meant not only that departments within the same institution might be in competition for the same students, but also that there was considerable animosity between neighbouring institutions offering similar courses. As one correspondence to the Technical Journal was moved to lament:

> One of the causes militating against the success of technical education has been the isolation of the teachers; the isolation of teachers in one department from teachers in other departments of the same institution; of teachers in one institution from another ... One of the objects of the Association is to break down the artificial barriers and wipe out the absurd and harmful jealousies between neighbouring institutions.[31]

The potential significance of such divisions amongst the staff is brought home when the size of these institutions is considered. In 1913, for example, there were 114 day technical schools with 1,050 full-time teachers, an average of nine teachers per school, and 27 technical institutes with 445 full-time teachers, an average of 17 per institution.[32] Though this is perhaps an underestimation of the number of teachers who might find themselves under the same roof, it is still a very small number indeed, especially when the departmental structure is taken into account. As late as the mid-thirties, Richardson estimated that there would be between three and six full-time assistants in a department in a large technical institute.[33] This might influence not only the individual teacher's ability to organise, but also his willingness to do so. Such small numbers would give him little immunity from his head of department or principal, the very members of the Association whose policies he would be opposing. Finally, such small numbers might mean that the chances of promotion were not that limited and failing promotion there was always the possibility of returning to their previous occupation. During the years of public expenditure cuts, for example, branch secretaries reported a mass exodus of teachers to industry.

THE LIMITS TO PROFESSIONALISM AS AN OCCUPATIONAL STRATEGY

Many social theorists have attached much theoretical importance to the development of the professions and their implications for both social structure and social change. Durkheim, for example, thought that professional organisations would create a new moral order, a solidarity which had hitherto existed only in pre-industrial societies and even then in mechanical form. The professions, he believed, 'should become so many moral milieux' bringing cohesion to a society 'lacking in stability whose discipline it is easy to escape and whose existence is not always felt'.[34] They were, then, a solution to the anomie which Durkheim diagnosed as the major ill of industrial societies. More recently Carr-Saunders and Wilson saw the professions as stabilising elements in society, providing the sense of power and purpose which had not been possible through an extension of democratic rights alone. The mechanism whereby the professions were to scale these heights lay in the ideal of altruistic service which these groups professed.[35] Tawney, for example, believed that in an 'acquisitive society' any community of interest had been subverted by individual self-interest and professionalism would be the major force for subjugating this rampant individualism to the needs of the community.[36] T.H. Marshall was concerned with exactly the same theme. In an attempt to redefine individualism, he tells us that 'it may mean the belief that the individual is the true unit of service, because service depends on individual responsibility which cannot be shifted onto the shoulders of others'. 'That,' he believed, 'is the essence of professionalism and it is not concerned with self-interest, but with the welfare of the client.'[37]

More recently still, Halmos has claimed that the professional service ethic is penetrating the ideologies of all groups and institutions in society, including those of business.[38] Another modern variation on the same theme emphasises the importance of specialist knowledge and skill in 'post-industrial' society and the power which professionals can achieve in their monopoly of such knowledge and skill. Unlike previous ruling classes, however, that power would be exercised in neither a coercive nor self-interested way but, by virtue of the service ethic, would be exercised for the good of the community as a whole. Veblen, for example, saw the professional engineer as the natural decision-maker in modern industrial society and argued that it would no longer be possible to leave the control of the industrial system in the hands of businessmen 'working at cross-purposes for private gain', rather it must be entrusted to 'suitably trained technological experts ... who alone are competent to manage it'.[39] But whatever the emphasis of the individual writer, in each case we arrive, as if by magic, at a post-capitalist, classless society, a society governed by consensus not conflict and organised for the social good, not individual self-interest.

The analysis of the ATTI during its early years demonstrates empirically the inadequacy of such an approach to the study of the professions, an approach which has been termed by Haug the 'knowledge-service-autonomy' model.[40] It is inadequate because it is based on two false assumptions. The first is related to the notion of altruistic service as opposed to self-interest. It has been seen that the impetus to association amongst technical, as indeed all, teachers was that of professional self-interest and their organisations gained momentum only to the degree that they were successful in their protective function. Indeed, as such, their aims were in essence little different from 'the selfish aims of class unionism' they were so careful to disavow. It is perhaps not going too far to say that those social theorists who saw in the development of professional associations the basis of a new social order were guilty of taking what might be called the rhetoric of professionalism at face value; of taking, as Elliott argues, 'professional ideology on trust'.[41] However, by far the most serious mistake made by the 'knowledge-service-autonomy' model has been the assumption that the power and autonomy achieved by the traditional professional associations is a real possibility for the myriad of specialised occupational groups which have grown up in more recent times. As Haug puts it, albeit to develop a different point, many of the social theorists who dealt with the professions based their estimate for the future on:

> two basic characteristics - mastery of knowledge and a humanitarian approach in the application of that knowledge: they do not, however, explicitly address the third core element of a profession: the

autonomy of the professional, his freedom from lay control in carrying out his occupational role, in a word, his power.[42]

It might be that this neglect of power as an important variable in determining the future of groups of professionals in society stems from a tendency amongst all these theorists towards a structural-functionalist position. Concentrating on the dysfunctional implications of unfettered individualism and self-interest in a society obviously divided by class, they seem to believe that the equally obvious need (from the functionalist point of view) for integration and consensus would automatically re-assert itself. It is ironic that whilst their concern for the future lay in a recognition of the social conflict inherent in a society dominated by a capitalist mode of production and its values, none of them embraced a class analysis of society which might lead to an examination of the crucial variable if we are looking for social change, that of the differential power of various groups in society to achieve it. Challenging their optimism, Haug, for example, asks:

> Will the professionalised society be ruled by the professionals as a concomitant of their monopoly over knowledge? Will the power lie in the hands of the expert who has access to scientific mysteries, advises the client for his own good and is backed by bureaucratic authority? Or are there other forces at work in a shifting battle for control in which the professional is likely to lose, in the end perhaps rendering the very concept of profession obsolete?[43]

The point is that there very definitely are such forces at work, the most important being that most professionals are no longer the independent practitioners of the old days, but salaried employees in a society which remains dominated by the economic laws of capital. No matter that the manager, for example, might have little authority in relation to the specialised work-task of the professional employee. As Friedson points out, the employer still sets the goals and allocates resources.[44] In other words, the manager may no longer have the authority, but as the representative of the employer, he still has the power. Whether the professional wants to increase either his salary or the quality of his service he is, in the final analysis, at the mercy of his employer like any other employee.

It might be argued that this is precisely why the older professions struggled to gain autonomy and why, in the early years at least, the professional model served as the ideal for the newly emerging professions. Indeed, the professional model was embodied in the first ever organisation of teachers, The College of Preceptors, established in 1846. Its members, the proprietors of the then numerous private schools and therefore independent in a very real sense, were concerned that the status of their profession was threatened by the growth of 'academies' of dubious repute. 'Schoolmasters,' they complained in their official history, 'were not very highly esteemed, and the more worthy were prejudiced by the evil repute of quacks and charlatans who looked upon school-teaching as nothing less than a mode of obtaining money under false pretences.'[45] Their aim was to become a self-governing profession much the same as the College of Physicians or the College of Surgeons and to this end they were the originators of the Teachers' Registration Movement, agitation for which began in 1860 but two years after the model, the General Medical Council, had been established by Act of Parliament. The College drafted a bill to be discussed by the Schools Inquiry Commission into Secondary Education in 1868, proposing a General Council for the teaching profession with powers to determine the qualifications necessary for registration and to sanction any teacher judged guilty of professional misconduct. The proposals for a Teachers' Register embodied in the Commission's report were not, however, such as to give the teachers effective control over their profession. Rather, they recommended an external test of efficiency which would bring the secondary schoolmaster more firmly under the control of the state.

As a result, barely a year after the Commission had reported, the Headmaster's Conference was set up to protect the interests of the better class of secondary school against encroachments by the State. Similarly, it was the reviving possibility of legislation in the field of secondary education which prompted the formation of the Incorporated Association of Headmasters and the Incorporated Association of Assistant Masters in 1890 and 1891 respectively. These associations represented the mass of schoolteachers in the lesser endowed schools which were threatened by the higher grade schools and whose interest therefore lay not in opposing state intervention but in promoting it. Whilst wanting public subsidy, however, they were anxious to preserve the traditional high status of secondary education and retain control in their own hands. The avowed aims of the Headmasters' Association, for example, were:

> to preserve the dominance of the Headmaster in all matters relating to the organisation of his school and hence limit any future powers accorded to Local Authorities as narrowly as possible and check the encroachments upon existing Secondary Schools of offshoots of School Boards and of the Technical Instruction Committees.[46]

In accordance with their as yet entrepreneurial status, they also aimed to set up a Professional Code which would condemn the practice of the payment of commissions for the introduction of pupils into their schools, the practice of advertising and, above all, the practice of wilfully under-bidding other schools.

On the other hand, the concerns of the National Union of Elementary Teachers (later to become the NUT) reflected very much their status as employees rather than independent professionals. It showed, in the opinion of Beatrice Webb at least, 'both in its objects and in its methods, a marked approximation to the Trade Union type'. Whilst it is doubtful whether the very early elementary teachers would have agreed with her, it is true that from the outset the NUET was more concerned with the more immediate trade union issues of salaries, pensions and conditions of service than with, for example, self-government through registration. Established in the year of the 1870 Elementary Education Act, their organisation developed in the context of the Revised Code of 1860 which instituted a system of payment-by-results. This had the effect of throwing the elementary teachers open to the laws of supply and demand without the government patronage they had hitherto enjoyed. The Revised Code itself was the product of an educational climate which considered that too much was being spent on education for the masses and that the elementary school teacher was himself being educated far above his proper station in life. 'You are the personal servants of the managers,' was the tenor of the official replies to deputations of teachers, 'they give you what wages they like, they can sack you when they choose, and they can require you to do any kind of work in and out of school hours.'[47]

A detailed examination of the fate of the Teacher's Registration Movement would indicate that it was precisely this employee status, actual in the case of the elementary teachers and imminent in the case of the secondary school teachers, which prevented the ideal of a self-governing profession ever becoming a reality for teachers. None of the proposals put forward by the State over a whole half-century came anywhere near the Registration Movement's ideal of a General Council to control entry into the profession and discipline its members. A second attempt was made in 1890 with two competing bills before Parliament. The first, Sir Robert Temple's bill, dealt only with secondary school teachers, proposing to set up a council modelled along the lines of the General Medical Council and governing, as Beatrice Webb put it, 'a little world of its own'. The NUT, however, would not contemplate a register which did not include themselves and a rival bill was put forward by Arthur Acland proposing a representative council for the whole profession, albeit with undefined powers, and a register of all teachers irrespective of grade or type of institution. This the secondary school teachers did not like and the whole question was again dropped. 1899, however, saw the setting up of the Educational Council, one of its jobs being the framing of regulations for a Teachers' Register and an Order of Council provided for its setting up in 1902.

This register was to be made up of two columns; Column A for teachers in elementary schools, Column B for teachers in secondary schools. The first column was effected simply by the Board of Education furnishing a list of all certificated teachers. The requirements for entry to Column B were such as to exclude all elementary teachers but to admit secondary school teachers on the easiest of terms. Any graduate, or indeed anyone who had passed with honours the Higher Local Examinations of Oxford and Cambridge could register, whether trained or not, on condition of three years teaching experience. Moreover, during the first four years of its operation, the registration authority had the power to admit anyone who had taught for ten or more years in any school other than elementary and the way was left open for any headmaster of a private school, whether qualified or not, to enter his name. Finally, this registration authority consisted of six nominees of the government and one representative each of the teachers' associations such that the criteria for entry rested firmly in the government's hands. Its consequent lack of power, funds insufficient to even publish the register and the persistent opposition of the NUT, who objected to what they saw as the second-class status of Column A, led to its 'voluntary' disabandonment in 1907. Opposition to the total abandonment of the ideal, however, led to legislation making it incumbent upon the Board of Education to constitute a Registration Council representative of the teaching profession which would itself be responsible for setting up a Register, this time consisting of one column only.[48]

It would seem then that the way was now clear for the teaching profession to become a self-governing profession. The great things which were expected of it were well summed up by the president of the Incorporated Association of Headmasters at their conference in 1914:

> For the first time in the history of the country we have a council thoroughly representative of the profession, not nominated by a Government Department, but chosen by the teachers themselves ... The Teachers' Registration Council gives us the only opportunity that has ever yet been placed within our reach of working out our own salvation, of struggling upwards from the chaos of mutual jealousies and conflicting interests, from the soul-destroying servitude of iron regulations into the order and freedom of a great, a united, and a self-governing profession.[49]

In the event, however, the powers conferred on the new Teachers' Registration Council were hardly such as to justify such enthusiasm. Although it was given the responsibility of forming and keeping a register of teachers who satisfied the conditions of entry established by the Council, it was given no power to enforce registration or to sanction those who would not, or could not, register. Thus the profession was still not closed to those it did not recognise. In fact, this had never been the intention of the Board of Education, the attitude of which had been made quite clear at the outset by Morant, then president, who, when asked whether the Board would make its grants conditional upon a governing body or local education authority requiring a substantial proportion of its teachers to be registered, replied that he was responsible to Parliament and Parliament alone. The terms upon which public monies were made available could not be dependent on the rulings of a professional body. As such, the Teachers' Registration Council was never of any real significance in the educational world and it passed quietly away with the passing of the Education Act of 1944.

The reasons why the powers of the Registration Council were so successfully restricted by the Board of Education were well summarised by Beatrice Webb when she pointed out that the vast majority of teachers no longer kept private venture schools, or taught private pupils. They were salaried employees entering into lasting contract of service with public bodies, subject to the control of Parliament and a government department. It seemed to her obvious that where such contracts existed 'it cannot be left simply to a combination of employees to dictate the legal qualification for the work, or even the conditions of service...This,' she argued, 'would in effect be tantamount to allowing the existing teachers to limit the number of professionals, and thus eventually control salaries and terms of service according to their own discretion.'[50] Even Carr-Saunders and Wilson, the very writers who saw such a bright future in the professional associations, recognised the limitations imposed on the Registration Movement by the teachers' employee status:

> No proposals with regard to teaching can have any immediate application which do not begin with the fact that most teachers are employed by the State ... so long as the State contributes to their salaries, it will refuse to delegate the duty of hall-marking to any special body. To delegate this duty to a body on which teachers sit would be to permit employees to say who should be employed.[51]

Neither was it the case that teachers were hampered by their special status as State employees. In discussing the case of journalists for example, Carr-Saunders and Wilson tell us that whilst the initial impulse to association was inspired by the traditional professional model, they were similarly unsuccessful in establishing any control over entry into their profession. It was precisely because of this that the Institute of Journalists failed, in the words of its own secretary, to satisfy the needs of the mass of journalists for a protective association and a break-away of younger men formed the more trade union-like National Union of Journalists in 1907. It is the argument of the following chapter that a similar failure in the tactics of the old guard of the ATTI led to their abandonment in favour of ones more trade union-like in character, albeit that this development took place at a much later date.

NOTES

1. In 1905, the Council of the London Association of Technical Teachers formally announced the extension of membership to teachers in the provinces. In 1906, Council reported that four local branches had been formed in West Yorkshire, West Lancashire, Manchester and District and Cornwall. Total membership at this point stood at 411 which, whilst low, represented a fair degree of 'completeness' given that the total number of full-time teachers in technical education stood at around 1,500. In the years before the Second World War, the Association remained very small. In 1922, for example, it could claim only 1,558 members of whom 23 per cent were part-time staff. By 1938, this number had risen to 2,027. In 1951, after the initial expansion of post-war technical education, the ATTI could still boast only 4,543 members. Thereafter membership figures increased rapidly to reach 12,671 in 1961 and 35,587 in 1971. In the year immediately before the merger with the Association of Teachers in Colleges and Departments of Education in 1975 membership stood at almost 50,000, some two-thirds of full-time lecturers in the public sector. By its tenth anniversary, NATFHE was claiming almost 80,000 members (including part-time) but it was beginning to suffer some small losses in full-time membership consequent upon the decline in the number of full-time teaching posts in the early eighties.

2. Quoted in Asher Tropp, The School Teachers (Heinemann, 1957), p.110.

3. Mrs. Sidney Webb, 'English Teachers and their Professional Organisation', Special Supplement in New Statesman, vol. V, 25 September 1915.

4. See, for example, Asher Tropp, 'Factors Affecting the Status of the School Teacher in England and Wales', where he uses the example of the school teacher to argue against the structural functionalist explanation of social

stratification put forward by Davis and Moore and shows that those periods when education has been accorded the highest priority (i.e. functional importance) in official circles have been precisely those periods when the school teacher has lost ground because the government has been able to manipulate teacher supply to its advantage.

5. Technical Journal, June 1910.
6. Ibid. February 1918.
7. Ibid.
8. Ibid. June 1935.
9. Quoted in H.C. Dent, Part-time Education in Great Britain (Turnstile Press, 1949), p.31.
10. Technical Journal, June 1921. The prejudices against which the ATTI was fighting were ably summed up in an article in the Technical Journal in 1923 where the writer argued forcibly that:

Technical education is not the teaching of trades ... does not specialise in the improvement of the manipulative skill of operators. Technical education is not a means of providing cheap labour for employers nor yet is it a method of relieving employers from the trouble of training their employees. Technical education is not a form of education designed for any one class of the community and it is not a form of education which limits participants to any particular class - it is not designed only for the artisan but equally for the captains of Industry.

11. C.T. Millis, Technical Education, Its Development and Aims (Arnold, 1925).
12. Royal Commission on University Education in London, First Report, 1910, pp.199-202.
13. Technical Journal, November 1915.
14. The strength with which the early leadership felt this commitment to technical education is nicely summed up in an official overview of the Association's work written by the ATTI in 1955 which finds a past president of the Association and secretary of the West Yorkshire Branch since 1927 quoting with approval a report given to the West Yorkshire Branch on the occasion of their amalgamation with London in 1906 which hoped 'to unite all Technical Teachers throughout the country in a strong bond of unity to the advantage and progress of Technical Education'. Mr Ing

adds that the history of the Association is 'the progressive embodiment of this hope in deeds'. The First Half Century (ATTI, 1955).

15. P. Elliott, The Sociology of the Professions (Macmillan, 1972), pp.14-22.

16. Quoted in ibid, p.15.

17. Quoted in Mrs Sidney Webb, New Statesmen, 1915.

18. These figures were given to the Annual Conference of the ATTI in 1911 and 1914 respectively.

19. Technical Journal, June 1912.

20. Ibid. June 1907.

21. Ibid. October 1917.

22. Ibid. June 1920. In his address to conference, the president of the Association reported that the rise in the cost of living during the war and over the years subsequent had been 155 per cent, the rise in technical teachers salaries but 30-40 per cent.

23. Ibid. June 1921.

24. Quoted in Tropp, The School Teachers, p.211.

25. Technical Journal, June 1923.

26. Quoted in Tropp, The School Teachers, p.209.

27. Ibid. p.156.

28. Ibid. p.209. Carr-Saunders & Wilson also comment on the success of the class teachers in getting the NUT to adopts its policies, especially during salary campaigns: 'whereas between 1870 and 1912,' they tell us, 'only two class teachers reached the highest office in the Union, between 1912 and 1921 only two head teachers became president. The days of its [the Federation of Class Teachers] greatest power were just before and just after the war during the salary crusade.' A.M. Carr-Saunders and P.A. Wilson, The Professions (Oxford University Press, 1933), p.256.

29. Correspondence with Mr Daniel Lloyd, 1975. Mr Lloyd started teaching in 1918 and was the first Principal of Stretford Technical College. He had been active in the ATTI since the twenties and President in 1935-6.

30. See, for example, excerpts from the Association's evidence to the Departmental Committee on Teachers' Salaries, quoted in the Technical Journal, August 1918:

> the range of the teaching in Technical Schools is very wide. At the one end the work is not far removed in standard from the elementary school, at the other end it is equal to that done in some

departments of the universities. There is almost a greater variety in the Institutions themselves. They vary from a continuation class held in an elementary school to such organisations as the Regent Street Polytechnic or the Manchester College of Technology ... [As for the teachers] some are fully occupied whole-time on work of university standing; others are artisans taken from the shops and likely to return to them; some are professional teachers whose chief work lies in the secondary and elementary school; others are engaged in important posts in Industry and Commerce and to them the salary they earn by teaching may or may not (sic!) be a matter of serious concern.

31. Technical Journal, October 1919.
32. Ibid. October 1913.
33. Richardson, The Technical College, pp.132-3.
34. Quoted in T.J. Johnson, Professions and Power (Macmillan, 1972), p.12.
35. Carr-Saunders and Wilson, The Professions, p.449.
36. R.H. Tawney, The Acquisitive Society (Fontana, 1966).
37. Quoted in Johnson, Professions and Power, p.13.
38. P. Halmos, The Personal Service Society, (Constable, 1970).
39. Quoted in Johnson, Professions and Power, p.13.
40. M.R. Haug, 'Deprofessionalization' in P. Halmos (ed), Professionalization and Social Change, 1973.
41. Elliott, Sociology of the Professions, p.139.
42. Haug, 'Deprofessionalization', p.195.
43. Ibid. p.196.
44. E. Friedson, 'Professionalization and the Organ-ization of Middle-Class Labour' in Halmos (ed), 1973.
45. Quoted in Mrs S. Webb, New Statesman, 1915.
46. Baron, 'The Secondary Schoolmaster', 1952, p.120.
47. Mrs S. Webb, New Statesman, 1915.
48. For these and other details see G. Baron, 'The Teachers' Registration Movement', British Journal of Educational Studies, May 1954.
49. Quoted in Mrs S. Webb, New Statesman, 1915.
50. Ibid.
51. Carr-Saunders and Wilson, The Professions, p.265.

4
The Transition

EARLY DEADLOCK

It has been argued that the ATTI was not a trade union in character during its early years and that whilst its very reason for being was to protect the interests of technical teachers, it neither saw itself as a trade union nor adopted normal trade union tactics in pursuit of those interests. Thus, whilst not performing the qualifying function of the traditional professional associations, it nevertheless embodied the 'institutionalised expression of status ideology' which Prandy, for example, argued to be the essence of the qualifying associations.[1] Its strategy was to enhance the status of technical teachers, not confront their employers over the negotiating table. In the face of salary cuts in 1931, for example, they 'unhesitatingly rejected' the use of sanctions of any kind and were even unwilling to engage in a press campaign as did the NUT. It was decided instead to continue their interviews with 'influential persons' in the hope of preventing the proposed cuts becoming law. In keeping with their self-image as professional gentlemen, the leadership continued to stand aloof from the trade union movement. In 1937 a motion from the London Division asking Council to consider asking trade union represent-atives to address members of conference was overwhelm-ingly defeated. The one mention of the TUC in the records of this period came as late as 1944 in the form of a branch request that the Executive should look into and advise on the question of affiliation. The idea was dismissed by the Executive as not in the best interests of the teachers. Thereafter, the issue was lost from sight until the sixties. During the thirties, at the same time as members were asking for fuller reports of Council meetings in the Technical Journal, others were complaining of its lack of professional interest and suggesting that its contents should, as far as possible, be calculated as to uphold the dignity of the Association. That both the Executive and Council were more in favour of the latter is apparent from Council's decision that the Assistant Secretary be empowered to delete passages from branch reports should they be considered, in his opinion, detrimental to the interests of the Association.

By way of contrast, the war years saw an increasing tendency to consider trade union issues more unashamedly in their own right. This time, the technical teachers demanded, and secured, not one but several war bonuses. Branch reports were dominated by two related bread and butter issues, over-time pay and part-time salaries. Resolutions were more demanding, less supplicating in tone and in 1944, the year of the Education Bill, only two out of twelve branches reported any discussion around its provisions. However, whilst more prepared to make trade union demands, the Association was still adamantly opposed to the use of trade union tactics and this can best be illustrated by developments on the salaries front over the succeeding years. In April 1944, Mr. R.A. Butler, Minister for Education, announced the constitution of two Burnham committees in place of the three which had been in existence in the pre-war years. The secondary and elementary committees were to combine to form the Burnham Main Committee to negotiate salaries for both secondary and primary school teachers. The Technical Committee remained intact. The ATTI and the NUT were represented on both committees because of the then close association between technical and school teachers' pay. The first Burnham Technical Report (1921) gave the technical teachers parity with the secondary school teachers and despite the increasing differentiation of technical teachers' salaries in the years following the war, they remained tied to the basic scale which was negotiated in the Main Committee.[2] The basic scale, however, was the scale now paid to the lowest grade of technical teacher and it is a comment on the changing nature of the technical teacher's job (as embodied in the increased volume of advanced-level work taught in the colleges) and his correspondingly enhanced status that a realistic salary goal in post-war years could be the complete separation of the technical from the school teacher scales. This goal was finally achieved in 1972.

Thus, perhaps the single most important provision in the 1945 Technical Report was the creation of the post of senior assistant in respect of advanced work, that is work deemed by the Burnham Committee to be of degree equivalence.

The Transition

Hitherto, its only recognition had been through a system of special allowances and this had not happened until 1937. So there were now two grades of technical teacher below that of a head of department, those of assistant and senior assistant, and the scales for the senior assistant were considerably higher than for the assistant, especially at the point of entry.[3] Despite this recognition of advanced work, the technical teachers were not entirely happy with the 1945 Report. Not all teachers involved with such work were to become senior assistants, rather then, as now, the number of posts at any one grade was to be determined by a complex formula calculated for the college as a whole. Despite registering its disappointment and regret, however, the Association found it necessary to remind its members of 'the power of the reasoned case'. 'Sound and fury,' emphasised the editor of the Technical Journal, 'are no substitute for carefully prepared and reasoned statements presented to the opposite panel ... and advocated by the leader of a well-informed panel of teachers. Salary settlements cannot be reached by epistolary contributions to the educational and general press.'[4] Even the pages of the Technical Journal were not considered the appropriate forum for such debate, for much the same reasons.

This behind closed doors policy of the Association did not achieve the desired results in 1948 when the second (post-war) Burnham Technical Committee reported. The differential between senior and other assistants had been increased and the assistantship scale lengthened. But the majority of technical teachers were neither senior assistants nor at the top of the assistantship scale. Conference and Council therefore saw resolutions calling for urgency on the question of the basic scale. Separation from the basic scale was the ideal, if not then a substantial increase was acceptable. In response to the strength of these resolutions, the Technical Journal saw fit to give a lecture on industrial relations:

> Negotiation implies accommodation and compromise if the negotiating machinery is to be effective and to remain in action ... Authorities and teachers view salary problems from different angles as do representatives of employers and employees in the real world. Those they represent may from time to time regard the negotiators on the other side as suffering from obliquity of vision

or wilful obstinacy in the face of facts which are, it seems to their respective constituents, so obvious and incontrovertible. The representatives of teachers, to be as successful as their constituents would like, must show that only by major amendments can an adequate and well-qualified teacher personnel be recruited. After each series of negotiations changes in salary structure are made, generally to the advantage of teachers. The pace may be slow but there is progress over the years towards an orderly solution.[5]

The 1951 Report brought some mitigation with the creation of four grades of lecturer; Assistants A and B, Lecturer and Senior Lecturer. It also wrote out the 1948 provision for special allowances for assistants and the fact that the number of senior assistants should be calculated in consultation with the Minister. Instead, Local Authorities would now determine the grading of posts under the guidance of Appendix VI of the Burnham Report.

Publicly, the Association was enthusiastic about the new report. The President in his address to conference that year described it as 'an imaginative outlook on the problem of catering for small institutions doing very elementary work and on large technical colleges undertaking a high proportion of work of university character and requiring teaching staff of the highest possible calibre in training and experience'.[6] He congratulated both panels on the scales they had recommended. Minutes of Council meetings, however, injected a private note of caution. There was already evidence that local authorities had not been exploiting to the full the possibilities for special allowances and senior assistants under the 1948 agreement and there was considerable suspicion that the technical teachers would not benefit as much as they should from the new salary scales given the increased local authority discretion provided for in the new Report. These suspicions did indeed turn out to be justified. The ATTI was not allowed access to the figures used to calculate establishments and at one point the local authorities actually specifically requested college principals not to release the appropriate figures to ATTI representatives. In the years immediately following the Report, branches were continually complaining about the implementation of Appendix VI. The interpretation of some local authorities brought forth the strongest words ever yet used by the Association of their employers and for the first time calls for the setting up of an independent body analogous to the University Grants Committee to finance public sector further and higher education.

It was such problems as these which plunged the Association into its first salary crisis in 1954. At a meeting of Council in November 1953, the provisions of the Burnham Main Report were accepted, the votes standing at 62 for, 36 against. Opposition to acceptance centred around the inadequacy of the proposed basic scale. But at a special Council meeting called to ratify the Burnham Technical Report, an Executive resolution to accept the offer was rejected by 56 votes to 53 and this was despite a plea from the Executive that should the agreement be rejected, there were no further steps they could take to induce the authorities to increase their offer. The Executive argued that rejection would not strengthen the hand of the teachers' panel and feared the humiliation of having to finally accept a previously rejected offer. The reasons for rejection were given in the Executive minutes as:

1. Insufficient increase offered to the higher grades

2. The possible detrimental manipulation of the proposed £100 allowance for Grade B Assistants

3. Non-differentiation between salaries of the Grade A Assistants and the basic scale of the Main Report

4. The absence of detailed guidance on the grading of posts.

Members active in the Association at the time remember the dispute as primarily one about the discretionary nature of the allowances. As one correspondent in the press argued the case:

> The first (discretionary allowance) is of a sum up to £100 to be paid to an Assistant Grade B who is considered by the Authority to carry responsibilities that make his scale pay inadequate ... Second is the sum of up to £30 to be paid as an addition to those second-class honours graduates in Grades A and B only, who seem to deserve it, according to

the Authority's decision. There is no certainty at all that these clauses would be interpreted in anything like the same way in different areas of the country. The burden of the decision will rest upon the governors who will be bound to call upon the advice of the principals and departmental heads in making up their minds and an aggrieved party may not, with all the best will in the world absolve his superior from all blame. In short the difficulties and dissatisfactions that must arise argue powerfully against any multiplication of difficulties that have already arisen in the assessment of grade ... A man ought to know what his salary is. It should depend as little as possible upon amorphous and ill-defined considerations. Our argument is that a way must be found to make such payments an integral part of the scales.[7]

In other words, the objections being raised were in relation to the 'particularism' which discretion can give rise to, increasing the dependence of the individual on his immediate superior rather than a straightforward entitlement to the 'rate for the job'. Similar objections were singled out in the operation of Appendix VI which was considered by the correspondent to be 'vague, ambiguous and phrased in the terminology of the Grammar School and University'.[8] The unfortunate result was that 'men with equal ability, responsibilities and standard of work, but employed by different authorities, may draw salaries varying by as much as £300 per annum, since a teacher's grading depends upon the whim, prejudice or enlightenment of the man responsible for the local interpretation of Appendix VI'.[9]

The ATTI's rejection of the 1953 Burnham Technical Report was the first time that a report had been rejected in the history of the Burnham negotiations and it is ironic that the traditionally gentlemanly, non-militant ATTI was the first teachers' association to do it. In doing so, the Association found itself in a position often faced by the trade union movement; negotiations had broken down. In such a situation, a trade union might consider sanctions to force management concessions. Not so the ATTI. In rejecting the Report, Council hoped simply to persuade management back to the negotiating table. When they refused, they were faced with a dilemma. Nothing was further from their minds than the possible use of sanctions. They went back to the management panel to ask them to re-open negotiations. They would not. Then to the Minister to ask if he would intervene on their behalf. He did not. Then a personal interview with the leader of the management panel, Sir William Alexander. At the point where the Minister refused to intervene, the Executive were willing to give in. One member argued that they should ask Council to reconsider their rejection on the grounds that they were 'being held up to ridicule'. Others feared that a prolonged failure to agree might wreck the Burnham Technical Committee. Should it 'fail', as they put it, the technical teachers might again be submerged into the Main Committee thus rendering negotiations for their sectional interests more difficult. All were convinced that the rank and file members were not behind rejection. However, many of the members of Council who were originally in favour of acceptance had by now changed their minds. The actions of the local authorities looked to them too much like dictation and one even spoke to the press of acceptance as 'immediate surrender with the uninviting prospect of any teachers' panel entering upon future negotiations immeasurably weakened'.[10] At a special Council meeting at the end of March, the vote for rejection had risen to 68, with 36 against.

It is important to note, however, that throughout the whole five month period of deadlock, during the latter part of which the technical teachers received no increase in salary, there was little talk of deviating from the traditional behind-closed-door strategy. There was certainly no talk of the possibility of the use of sanctions. One group of teachers from Middlesbrough did address an open letter to the Executive which they circulated to all branches. It contained resolutions to the effect that all the four grievances cited above should form the basis of new negotiations and that a publicity campaign be immediately launched to obtain the support of all those interested in technical education. Most significantly, it demanded that the membership appoint a teachers' panel 'which believes in the justice and practicability of these proposals and is prepared to carry on a fight for their realisation'.[11] Nothing came of it, however. Indeed, the former General Secretary of the Association who had been an active 'rejectionist' during the dispute told the writer that 'there wasn't a cat in hell's chance of getting any action though we were passing motions here and there to try and get support. But there just wasn't the basis'. Finally, after another approach to the Minister and a further refusal on the part of the management to re-open negotiations, the Executive proposed again to Council that the original award be accepted. Though the Management Panel had refused to re-open negotiations on the whole of the claim, there had been suggestions that a meeting might be possible provided that the salary scales in the provisional agreement were accepted. The final agreement provided for modifications to Appendix VI on the grading of posts and the deletion of discretionary allowances and was accepted by Council in July, approximately five months after the original offer had been rejected. The militants in the Association might well have been in the minority at this time, but that they were a growing minority is indicated by the fact that six divisions voted against acceptance of the now modified report.

Indeed, what is interesting about this whole episode is that for the first time the lines were beginning to be drawn between the old-guard in the Association and the up-and-coming trade unionists. The old-guard, for example, defined the problem as one of a breakdown of the Burnham machinery. The source of dissatisfaction lay in that should agreement not be reached, there was no mechanism whereby the teachers could re-open negotiations except by the consent of management. Should there continue to be deadlock, there was no provision for arbitration unless by consent of both panels. Further, the salary scales finally agreed were payable under a statutory order issued by the Minister (who himself had the power of veto) and it was not possible to pay salaries in accordance with the new scales earlier than the date of the order itself. All these factors did, of course, put the technical teachers at a disadvantage in negotiations, but it was a disadvantage, others pointed out, which was little different from that of other employees in negotiation with their employers. 'The teachers,' they argued, 'merely found themselves in a position frequently met in all types of salary and wage negotiations, viz: that the side holding the purse strings says that it has made its final offer ... this is not a breakdown [of the Burnham negotiating machinery] and teachers should realise that they do not enjoy a privileged position in salary negotiations.'[12]

FOR TRADE UNIONISM

> People, particularly in the ranks of the NAS, have been heard to say that the ATTI is nothing more than the Technical College Branch of the NUT. Whatever the truth of this may have been in the past the ATTI now seems to be developing into the more militant and, dare one say it, the more interesting union.
>
> <u>Times Education Supplement</u>, 17 June 1966

Opposition to the timidity of the leadership's policies began to rise in the 1950s. In 1955 and 1956 demands were made for an interim award to cover the rise in the cost of living and a motion of censure from one division called for the resignation of any ATTI representative on the teachers' panel who in any way impeded the progress of such an award. Another division urged an immediate national salary campaign and asked that a special Council meeting be called whenever Burnham negotiations reached a stage requiring variations in the policy laid down by the national conference. Others still were concerned to avert a repetition of the paralysis which followed the rejection of the 1953 provisional agreement and asked the Executive to prepare a plan of action to be implemented in the event of a future breakdown. The Executive began to lose its influence on the Council. In 1957 Council rejected a dependents' pension scheme against the wishes of the Executive. The issue was one of who should contribute and the arguments for and against neatly sum up the different orientations of the old and new-guard in the Association. For acceptance, the Executive argued that there was no hope of getting anything better in the near future; the need was urgent and the scheme was actually just. Those arguing against believed that the consequent shortage of teachers would force the local authorities into reconsidering; to accept was to deny the power of the teachers' associations to influence public opinion and if the civil servants and police could have a shared-cost scheme, why not the teachers?

Thus, there was in the arguments of the new-guard an increasing unwillingness to compromise over important issues combined with an optimism about the potential power of the teachers' associations which was in clear distinction from the peculiar mixture of conciliation and defeatism which had long characterised the stance of the ATTI. Nevertheless, it was not until the early sixties when the fiercest battles over salaries had to be fought that we see any explicit demands for the use of sanctions in pursuit of Association goals. The turning point would seem to have been 1961. The provisional agreement negotiated in the Burnham Main Committee was rejected by the NUT Executive in early June. At the Summer Council, the ATTI moved acceptance but after considerable debate the motion was largely lost. The NUT decided in favour of sanctions in pursuit of their claim at a special Conference in June. By the time the Burnham Committee reconvened, however, the Chancellor of the Exchequer had announced a pay pause and the Minister of Education rejected both the size and the distribution of the proposed (non-ratified) agreement. The provisional agreement had involved a sum of £47 million but the Minister refused to contemplate a sum bigger than £42 million. He was further concerned that the salary differentials contained in the provisional agreement be retained or even increased within this now significantly reduced global sum, a blow to both the NUT and the ATTI committed as they were to a substantial increase on the basic scale. More sinister still, there were also proposals to reconstitute the Burnham Committees to allow for ministerial views being made known at a much earlier stage in the negotiations. The teachers' panel moved quickly to accept the previously rejected provisional agreement but the Minister remained firm and sanctions were again proposed at a special NUT Conference early in September. A one-day strike, selected strikes and sanctions involving withdrawal of goodwill were all considered but in the event ballots held in the areas expected to undertake such action showed only a bare majority in favour. Seriously divided throughout, the NUT abandoned its plans for direct action and the teachers' panel accepted what would have otherwise been an imposed settlement.[13]

What is interesting about the whole episode is that the ATTI was no longer united in opposition to the NUT's proposed use of sanctions. At a special Council meeting in October there was even a resolution in favour of a one-day strike of ATTI members in support of the NUT. Whilst largely lost, the Executive did recommend that those ATTI members directly affected by NUT action should consider similar action 'according to their conscience'. This in itself brought a storm of protest from some divisions demanding to know how this could be reconciled with the Conference decision of that year to fully support any NUT action, including strike action. The Executive replied that it was Council, not Conference which was the governing body of the Association, a much different interpretation of the rules from that given some years earlier when it had been agreed in the Executive that a resolution from two divisions to the effect that 'Annual Conference shall lay down the general policy of the Association' be not considered on the grounds that 'this has been the policy of the Association since its inception'.[14]

This new interpretation of the rules might have had something to do with the fact that the minority of militants on Council could now rely for support on a majority of militants at Conference and the Executive was afraid of losing its hitherto unassailable position. Nevertheless, it should be emphasised that the Executive itself had come a long way along the trade union road since the early days of the Association and it might even be argued that at this stage far from being ideologically opposed to the use of sanctions, they were, like the NUT, simply practising the art of the possible. At the special Council meeting in October, for example, the General Secretary considered it his duty to inform the delegates that there were indications of 'a considerable measure of disturbance amongst teachers in further education who were apparently not inclined to withdrawal of labour, even for one day'.

However, government intervention in salary negotiations over the next two years occasioned a significant change in the public stance of the ATTI. In 1961 one of the arguments against the use of sanctions had been that if the Minister's proposals were accepted, this would encourage him to postpone any reform of the Burnham machinery which gave him greater say in negotiations. In the event, the teachers gained little from this concession. In 1963, the Minister refused to ratify provisional agreements reached in both the Main and the Technical Committees on the grounds that more money should be made available for teachers with longer service, higher qualifications and greater responsibility, in other words, widening yet again differentials within the teaching profession. Unlike the NUT, the ATTI was not at this stage against the widening of differentials as such, though it did object to the fact that given the existence of a global sum, the Minister's proposals to give money to the higher grades had the effect of taking it away from the lower. It was not the Association's aim, however, to quibble about the particular amendments the Minister had made to the Report. Rather, it was vehemently opposed to ministerial interference in what it called 'the elementary rights of wages' negotiations'. Indeed, it was against this background that in 1963 the presidential address to conference delivered a strong, fighting speech upholding the basic trade union right to free collective bargaining:

> there is the question of freedom, which in this country is our birthright ... Surely this applies also to collective bargaining which freedom includes the right to argue a case with the employer, the right to withdraw labour or withhold payment, and above all the need to honour the final handshake. Teachers have never easily contemplated, nor tried to use, the sanctions of collective bargaining, usually to their cost ... and this in a day and age when strike has become a household word.[15]

But perhaps what is most significant here is the explicit recognition that teachers' interests might not have been best served by the quiescent tactics hitherto employed and the implicit recognition of an identity of purpose between the teachers' associations and the wider trade union movement.

This speech marks the beginning of a qualitative change in the character of the Association from that of a status-conscious professional association to an organisation conscious and proud of its identity as a trade union. The first formal recognition of this change came in 1964 when conference decided to change the order of the Association's aims and objectives. The protective rather than education function was now to be given priority. The birth of this new trade union was not without its complications, however. As early as 1959, the old guard within the Association had sensed the direction of change and had proposed at Conference a motion to the effect that 'the full participation of this Association in the development at all levels of policies for technical and further education is no less important than its representation of the interests of its members in their salaries and conditions of work'.[16] It was largely carried. In January 1965, after the rule change, these same people called a special Council meeting in the hope of reversing the decision. According to the reports in the Technical Journal, this meeting was turbulent, but the trade unionists won the day. 'Have we a guilt complex,' asked one delegate, 'are we ashamed of being a trade union?'[17] The answer was apparently not and the amendment was lost, but only by a narrow majority.

Further formal recognition of this new-found status came a year later with affiliation to the TUC, the first teachers' association to do so. Affiliation to the TUC had first been proposed at Conference in 1962 but was withdrawn in favour of a resolution instructing the Executive to prepare an 'impartial' memorandum on the whole question. This it did to January Council in 1964. Whilst fulfilling its commitment to impartiality by making no recommendation the report did seem to indicate a favourable attitude. No disadvantages to affiliation were listed and the institutional autonomy of the TUC from the Labour Party was stressed. So too were the educational activities of the TUC and its involvement with the National Economic Development Committee. It was not until 1966, however, that resolutions in favour of affiliation gained sufficient priority from the divisions to be discussed at conference. The resolution was carried with 115 votes in favour, 56 against. The Executive moved an amendment that a referendum of all members be held on the question but this was defeated, 71 votes in favour, 87 against. Once again the old guard tried to reverse the decision by calling a special Conference. This time, however, the Executive moved the resolution for immediate affiliation without a referendum which, much to the surprise of the old guard, was carried by an even bigger majority with 157 votes in favour, 68 against. By the same token, an amendment proposing a referendum was heavily lost. Asked why it had changed its position to immediate affiliation without referendum, the Executive replied that an Executive which did not support conference decisions was 'not worth much', an interesting reversal of earlier positions when the sovereignty of Conference had been very much challenged.[18] But then the compositon of the Executive itself had changed significantly over the previous two years, with the new guard in the Association now predominating even there.

THE SIGNIFICANCE OF TUC AFFILIATION
Writers concerned to assess the significance of white-collar workers in the occupational structure of advanced capitalist

societies have been much concerned with the character of their associations. Routh, for example, set the parameters of the early debate well when he argued that traditionally, the white collar had been 'the symbol of respectability, the mark of moderation'. The white collar, he continued 'was the guarantee of its owner's conservatism, of that unswerving loyalty to the status quo that qualified him as the custodian of the firm's secrets and set him apart from the muscle-using process worker and craftsman. For those who saw the need for social improvement, this had serious consequences. Would the growth in the proportion of white-collar workers in the economy 'entail a slowing down of progress - in particular the transformation of the trade union movement into a docile appendage of the personnel department?'[19]

At work, the traditional white-collar employee was seen as a promotion conscious, pro-management individualist. Sykes, for example, has argued that clerks:

> want to 'get on' as individuals; they want promotion; they act individually and set the highest value on individuality; they think it right and proper to do what benefits them personally, not what benefits clerks as a whole. Thus their interests lie in raising their own status as individuals, not working through a trade union to raise the status of all clerks. The way in which they do this is by competing for promotion in the office, and by improving their individual status through securing educational or professional qualifications at night school or by private study. This entails dealing directly with the employer and striking individual bargains with him on pay and conditions ... [20]

In broader terms, the white-collar, worker was the embodiment of what Prandy has termed 'status ideology', an ideology which comprises an essentially 'harmonistic' view of society made up of status groups not classes in conflict. Thus, those who hold a 'status ideology' see society as:

> a set of superior and inferior grades in which every member accepts the validity of the status criteria, and thus his own place within the hierarchy. Status stratification is essentially harmonious, in the sense that it arises out of an acceptance of the

authority structure. Individuals can compete with each other to raise their own status, but the validity of the criteria by which status is measured, the bases of legitimation, are not questioned.[21]

And it was this status ideology which was seen as the explanation as to why white-collar workers were reluctant to join trade unions. Trade unionism, it was argued, is based upon unity and collective action. Thus, to join a union would entail a consciousness on the part of the white-collar worker which was totally alien to his being. Strauss, for example, argued that for white-collar workers to join a union meant 'abandoning hope', 'showing hostility to the boss' and 'throwing away all opportunity to forge ahead on merit'.[22]

The fact remained, however, that many groups of white-collar workers had long been organised and that, even at this time, they were becoming increasingly so. In the face of this reality, the focus of the debate shifted from the reluctance of white-collar workers to join a union to the analysis of what impact such factors might have on the character of their organisations. The differences which were found to exist between the traditional manual workers' unions and white-collar associations were taken to be a symptom of their different class positions: the traditional trade unions were taken to be an expression of the objective class position of manual workers and a consciousness, however imperfect, of class interest; white-collar associations being organisations of 'middle class' workers were taken to be the embodiment of status consciousness. It was at this point that the idea that there is no necessary relationship between unionisation and the development of class consciousness was born. 'It is important to realise', said Lockwood, 'that action in concert while obviously an expression of group consciousness is not necessarily an expression of class consciousness.'[23]

This was indeed found to be so in the early years of the ATTI. Underlying both the strategy and tactics of the Association lay a 'harmonistic' view of both employment relations and of class relations in the wider society. The collective forces of the technical teachers, such as they were, were mobilised to raise the status of the profession within the wider status hierarchy, not to confront the employer over the negotiating table. Indeed, rather than recognise a conflict of interest, the ATTI went out of its way to erect a unity. It is for this reason that the concept of status ideology as described by Prandy must be modified, for it is not necessarily as passive a phenomenon as he implied. Rather, as has been seen from the early activities of the ATTI, the validity of the criteria by which status is judged can be challenged and it is precisely this possibility which gives rise to collective organisation amongst status-conscious employees. Thus, rather than see the distinctive features of status as opposed to class consciousness in terms of the two separate dimensions of 'harmony vs conflict' and 'individualism vs collectivism', the two dimensions need not be distinct.[24] Rather, the ATTI in its early years might best be described as the embodiment of what shall be called harmonistic collectivism.

It is true then that the ATTI, whilst protective in function, could not be called a trade union if trade unions are to remain the class organisations many writers have taken them to be. Lockwood argued that the fundamental defining characteristic of trade unions as class organisations is that in strategy and tactics they embody the principles of 'class opposition' (the conflict of interest inherent in employer/employee relationships) and 'class unity' (the identity of interest with other employees as employees). Thus, 'in the case of black-coated workers, class-consciousness may be said to emerge when the members of a clerical association realise first that their common interests are engendered by the conflict of interest between employer and employee and, secondly, that their common interests are not fundamentally dissimilar in type from those underlying the concerted actions of manual workers'.[25] With regard to the measurement of class consciousness, he argued that it could be traced 'in a variety of indirect ways': for example, 'by a change in the name and purposes of the association ... by the adoption and use of certain types of sanctions, such as strike action for the attainment of its goals; by the affiliation of the association to the wider trade-union movement; by its identification with the political wing of the Labour Movement; by sympathetic behaviour in critical class situations, such as the General Strike; as well as the general social and political outlook of the membership and leaders of the association'.[26]

Blackburn, too, saw trade unions as essentially class organisations. Concerned to test the hypothesis that white-collar workers will only join trade unions if they are 'respectable', a logical conclusion if white-collar workers are the pro-management individualists many have believed them to be, he developed the concept of 'unionateness' as a measure of union character. His measures of 'unionateness' were not dissimilar to Lockwood's indices of class conscious- ness and approximated closely to the characteristics of the traditional manual trade unions. Thus his measures of trade union character were:

1. It (the union) regards collective bargaining and the protection of the interests of members as its main function.

2. It is independent of employers for purposes of negotiations.

3. It is prepared to be militant, 'using all forms of industrial action which may be effective'.

4. It declares itself to be a trade union.

5. It is registered as a trade union.

6. It is affiliated to the TUC.

7. It is affiliated to the Labour Party.[27]

Others writing at about the same time isolated one or other of these characteristics as important indices of character. Routh, for example, discussing the new-found militancy of many white-collar associations argued that 'the attitude to direct action is not the only test by which the quality of a union may be judged. There are also questions of affiliation to the Trades Union Congress and to the Labour Party.'[28]

These then were the parameters of the early debate about the significance of white-collar unionism. In so far as a white-collar association came to take on a significant proportion of these characteristics, it was argued that it, too, had become a class organisation; that it had become, or was in the process of becoming, what Lockwood termed 'a whole-hearted' trade union. Since then the whole concept of 'unionateness' has come under attack from a variety of sources. Some have questioned the extent to which the criteria constitute adequate and unambiguous measures of union character, others its unidimensionality and inability to distinguish more subtle differences in job regulation and control. More specifically, there is the problem of the extent to which 'unionateness' can be equated with class consciousness. In this respect, the symbolic significance of affiliation to the TUC has been singled out for special attention. It has been argued, for example, that far from involving a felt identity of interest with the wider labour movement, affiliation might be purely instrumental in nature. Bain and his colleagues argue that a union's decision to affiliate is 'often motivated more by its organisational needs than by its degree of commitment to "the general principles and ideology of trade unionism".'[29] Equally, strikes and other forms of militant action need not necessarily be an indicator of class consciousness since they 'can very often be for sectarian ends and contribute nothing to wider class or even union goals'.[30] The argument is reminiscent of C. Wright Mills' comment on the individual white-collar worker:

> In the union or out of it, for it, against it, or on the fence, the white-collar employee usually remains ... the little individual scrambling to get to the top, instead of a dependent employee experiencing unions and accepting unions as a collective means of collective ascent. This lack of effect ... is of course linked with the reason white-collar people join them: to most members, the union is an impersonal economic instrument rather than a springboard to new personal, social and political ways of life.[31]

So too, in the TUC or out of it, the white-collar association remains the status-conscious, pro-management appendage to the personnel department it has always been said to be!

Such a position has been argued specifically in relation to the teachers' associations by both Coates and Manzer. Respectively, they see TUC affiliation and teacher militancy as the product of the search for 'optimal strategies' given certain changes in the organisational environment, in this case the breakdown of the close, informal and co-operative relations which existed between the teachers' unions, their employers and the government in the immediate post-war years. Coates, for example, argues explicitly that:

> TUC affiliation tells us little, if anything, about

the changing consciousness of class amongst union-
ised teachers, but much about the changing
structure, policy and accessibility of Government
faced by teachers' associations in the 1960s. Even
teacher militancy, which is certainly more reliable
an indicator of membership attitudes, cannot fully
be explained without reference to the pattern of
Government policy against which militant action
was taken.[32]

Both Coates and Manzer are undoubtedly correct in their
analysis of the immediate impetus to both TUC affiliation
and teacher militancy. They are also correct when they
point out that the teachers' associations did not seek affiliation until after the government had refused to consult the
Conference of Professional and Public Service Organisations
(COPPSO), an alliance of white-collar associations including
the NUT and the ATTI set up specifically to express the
views of white-collar employees (especially those in the
public services) to government agencies over incomes
policy. Indeed the arguments used by the activists in the
ATTI in favour of TUC affiliation would seem to reinforce
the importance of the teachers' impotency in the face of
government incomes policy as a major factor. Explaining the
reasons for affiliation to a special Conference called in the
hope of reversing the decision, the General Secretary spoke
of how incomes policy was being decided between the TUC,
the government, and CBI and that they had to operate
within that framework to get the best they could. Like
others, he also emphasised TUC involvement in industrial
training, an issue of crucial importance to the
Association.[33] When affiliation was first formally proposed
at Conference in 1965, the speech in favour was limited
almost entirely to educational issues. In similar vein, care
was taken to separate the 'industrial' from the 'political'
ends of the TUC, 'political' ends signifying party political
support for the Labour Party.[34]

In spite of all this, however, it was obvious to anyone
involved in the ATTI during this period that the issue was
not a purely pragmatic one. The issue was about the proper
nature and function of the Association. Was it to remain
trapped within the confines of status professionalism or was
it to become a fully-fledged trade union? This was summed
up in a speech at the special Conference in favour of a
referendum on the issue, because the Association, it was

argued, 'embraced a large number of members whose outlook was a strictly professional one and who, politics apart, were against a step which emphasised the trade union function of the Association'.[35] In reply, another activist threw down the gauntlet. 'We have to decide, ' he told Conference, 'whether to cling to the nineteenth century ideas of professional status or whether to involve ourselves in the affairs of the nation.'[36] In other words, whilst the arguments mustered in favour of TUC affiliation were pragmatic in content, the debate was taking place within a context which was very definitely ideological in character and it is only within the context of this larger debate that the significance of TUC affiliation can be properly understood.

The extremes of this debate were aptly set out in correspondence to the Technical Journal. On the one side was a letter in 1963, soon after TUC affiliation was first broached:

> One of the aims of the ATTI is to 'Promote and safeguard the professional interests of the teacher', one part of this promotion of professional interests is surely to advance the professional status of the technical lecturer generally and eventually aim to raise it to the same level as Doctors, Dentists, Solicitors, etc. With this in mind we would like to comment on the proposed affiliation to the TUC.[37]

The letter continues as if to jutaxpose these high-status reference groups with the low-status of the membership of the TUC:

> The number of non-manual workers in the affiliated unions is less than 12 per cent of the total of affiliated union members, of these a very much smaller proportion could be called professional: if we affiliated we could first be made to associate with ideas that were not to our advantage and secondly to associate with a large number of other union members whose aims and interests are not compatible with ours.[38]

On the other side was a letter in 1966, just before the original decision to affiliate:

> Since the first interference in the Burnham machinery by the last Government, there has been a progressive limitation on free negotiations between teachers and education authorities. With the present settlement salaries are now definitely awarded by dictation ... Teachers in further and higher education must realise that they are no longer part of an elite (if ever they were) treated respectfully by our ruling class. The ATTI must therefore cease to be a 'respectable' body relying for satisfactory settlement on closed discussion with management. Such closed discussion may be best in settling individual cases, but in the matter of national salary scales our leaders must learn to use the well-tried trade union methods, particularly rousing the membership into public activity and the consideration of industrial action.[39]

And doubtless there were numerous positions in between.

CLASS UNITY

> The ATTI has lived up to its reputation as the most consciously trade union of all teacher unions when two strongly worded motions condemning government policy on pay in the public sector and the Industrial Relations Act were passed by conference with scarcely a vote against.

> Times Higher Education Supplement, 2 June 1972

The history of the ATTI shows that at least some of the criteria of 'unionateness' did constitute landmarks in the ATTI's development from a gentlemanly professional association to a more trade union-like body. Furthermore, it would seem that preparedness to take industrial action and affiliation to the TUC were crucial indices of this change in character; industrial action being a measure of a felt conflict of interest between employers and employees and affiliation to the TUC being, in Blackburn's words, 'the most direct way of expressing shared interests and identity with other unions'.[40] Subsequent developments would seem to confirm this intepretation of events. The ATTI was implacably opposed to any form of incomes policy and by the late sixties public sector workers in particular were being hit harder than most. The teachers were no exception. For example, 1967 saw deadlock in the Burnham Committee and an arbitration award which conceded nothing in terms of salary structure. The NUT was already operating sanctions short of strike action in support of its own claim and in October of that year Council called upon the Executive 'to take strong action, including a ballot for sanctions, to bring home to the management side of the Burnham Further Education Committee and the government, the need to improve the offer, as well as to show solidarity with the NUT in our common struggle'.[41] In the event, however, the arbitration award was accepted albeit with the threat that it was 'not an end, but a beginning to a new phase of stronger pressure by teachers', the college lecturers entering this phase 'with the strength added from the gains achieved by their NUT colleagues in their recent resolute action'.[42] Also, the arbitrators had sympathised with the Association's concern over the lower end of the scales and the ATTI thought this encouraging for the next round of negotiations. These took place in May 1969 and saw a management offer of 6 per cent in the face of an 18 per cent claim with no significant movement on structure. An Executive resolution to May Council to reject the offer was carried substantially as was a further resolution from London Division instructing the Executive to initiate a press campaign and organise a national lobby of the House of Commons. It also instructed the Executive to consider a national one-day strike and other forms of withdrawing labour together with the establishment of a strike fund. The claim went to arbitration in July and in September the teachers heard the results: the management offer had been allowed to stand with only minor alterations.

Whilst the lobby of Parliament took place prior to arbitration in July, the ATTI never did come to take action on its own behalf. This was at least in part due to the fact that the Association was overtaken somewhat by events in the Burnham Main Committee. In February 1969, an NUT special Conference had accepted the management offer of 6 per cent only to have that decision effectively overturned by an annual Conference at Easter which bound the NUT Executive to submit an interim claim of £135, to be operative from 1 April 1970. The subsequent campaign for the interim award came eventually to involve the school teachers in a series of stoppages over a ten-month period, culminating just before settlement in the commencement of indefinite strikes and the threat of an invigilation ban. When the interim claim was put to the Burnham Main Committee in October 1969, the ATTI gave its full support on the grounds of their own 'deep dissatisfaction with the FE arbitration award, and the crippling context of the Prices and Incomes Policy, which formed a straitjacket preventing real negotiation on the further education claim'.[43] It also meant that the ATTI would press for any interim award granted to the school teachers to be applicable to further education.

Subsequent events are perhaps best described in the words of an Executive report in the Technical Journal:

> The derisory £50 offered by the management in response to the £135 interim claim in the Burnham Primary and Secondary Committee, and its instant rejection by the teachers' side has been swiftly followed up by half-day strikes of local teacher associations. As we go to press, the Inner London teachers have announced that they will be out on strike on 20 November, and similar action is taking place and planned all over the country.
>
> As a result of such wage increases as those won by the firemen and the dustmen, the organisations representing teachers in schools have, in response to the unmistakable will of their members, come to take the ATTI view of prices and incomes policy as applied to teacher salaries which led ATTI representatives on the Burnham Main earlier this year to vote against acceptance of the award. The Association presented its own claim in mid-November, but even before then gave its full support to NUT local action. An Executive statement to branches shortly after the Burnham meeting of 10 November expressed solidarity with the Union, and told branches that they were free to join in with half-day stoppages in co-operation with the local NUT associations if invited.[44]

In addition, the Executive recommended that ATTI members should voluntarily pay to the NUT the same levy as they were asking of their own members 'to help sustain colleagues in schools who are fighting the battle for everyone in education'.[45] As a response to these calls to support

112

the school teachers, nearly 160 ATTI branches involving some 5,000 members joined local NUT associations in day or half-day strike action. Forty more branches gave donations to the NUT sustentation fund in lieu of striking and by the beginning of January estimated ATTI contributions to the fund were between £30,000 and £40,000.

Neither was this support purely 'instrumental' in nature. The stand taken by the ATTI leadership throughout was undoubtedly ideological in content. They interpreted the teachers' ultimate victory in terms of a 'radical change in the balance of forces between employers and employed',[46] and talked of a new found solidarity and consciousness of strength which would from that time on prevent the local authorities and the government treating the teacher with contempt. From the beginning they challenged government incomes policy and saw the NUT's eventual rejection of the 6 per cent as an indication that the school teachers had 'begun showing a healthy unwillingness to accept government policies as immutable'.[47] Consequently, they were not concerned to make a special case for teachers but rather thought that 'united action by the teachers should help to put the government's incomes policy where it belongs - in the dustbin'.[48] Significantly, Edward Short, then Minister for Education and himself an NUT member, tried to divert the teachers from the course of industrial action with the promise of self-government through a newly-constituted Teachers' Council. The terms he used are significant in their constant juxtapositon of professionalism and trade unionism:

> I want to discuss the question as to whether or not we are right after all to pursue the goal of professional status or whether the time has come to regard the work of the teacher in industrial terms. For there is a difference and I do not think you can have it both ways ... Around you, in other walks of life, you see workers' conditions spelt out in exact detail; rights insisted upon, responsibilities delineated and restricted, and not infrequently, sectional interests or motives of private gain pursued relentlessly, without much thought about the consequences to others. It is small wonder that the temptation to follow suit is strong, and of course many teachers believe that in the competitive atmosphere of today their own social status and economic standing are bound to

113

> deteriorate unless they too invoke similar methods...
> Phrases such as 'industrial action' have to me an odd ring against the background of the teachers' past record of service to society and their claim to professional status, and as the minister responsible to Parliament for the whole education service I must ask myself what is the effect of such phrases, and of some of the accompanying actions upon the pupils.[49]

The ATTI was quick to respond. Referring to the Teachers' Council as a 'rather aged carrot', the president in his address to conference that year attacked these arguments in no uncertain terms. Had teachers been more willing to take industrial action in the past, he argued, and less willing to cling to professional respectability and hide behind responsibilities to the young, they might have got a better deal for themselves and their charges.[50]
Not surprisingly, however, there were some amongst the membership who wanted to cling to these last vestiges of professional respectability and the issue of strike action was hard-fought in some branches. For example, one branch officer described these months as a very tense period; in his branch there had been a narrow majority in favour and even once the decision had been taken, many lecturers still did not come out on strike. At another college, the branch had been split right down the middle:

> It was a bitterly fought issue. The branch was totally divided. We had four ballots, two secret, two at open meetings. The decisions fluctuated but eventually crystallised into a definite majority. About half to three-quarters of the membership stayed away, better than we expected but less than we had hoped for. Some people came out who had originally voted against.[51]

After the event, there was evidence of considerable bitterness on both sides of the divide, with strikers calling for the expulsion of those who failed to support them and non-strikers threatening resignation if they could not follow the dictates of their own conscience without victimisation. The Executive trod carefully, emphasising that whilst they had hoped members would decide in favour of strike action, it remained only a recommendation not an instruction and they refused to take the action against non-strikers which some branches were demanding.

As a result, the following year demands for a closed-shop reached the agenda of conference as an explicit attack on the individualism of those who had claimed 'freedom of conscience' during the strikes. 'The time had come,' argued the proposer of the motion for a closed shop 'when it should be a condition of employment that teachers belong to an appropriate union; if they did not wish to go in under these conditions, they had the individual freedom to look for another job.' 'People were coming in,' he continued, 'who had never belonged to any union, reaping the benefits of forty years of union work done by other people. They refused to come out on strike, they refused to pay the levy - but they didn't refuse the £120.'[52] 'What sort of conscience is it,' asked the ex-president in his speech in favour, 'that permits other people to fight their battles for them?'[53] In the event, however, an amendment was carried on a card vote asking the Executive to prepare more detailed plans to be presented at the next Conference. It was argued that this would also give time to test the feelings of the membership in the branches.

That some amongst the membership were not slow to show their feelings could be seen from correspondence in the educational press. One such correspondent is worth quoting at some length:

> The recent decision ... to prepare a detailed plan of how a 'closed-shop' in further education colleges might be achieved makes one ask why such a trivial matter should even be tabled by such a 'professional body of people' at an annual conference.
>
> To answer this question it is necessary to admit to the ever-widening division of staff in further education colleges between those who see their work in the light of a profession and those who see their work as a 9am to 5pm job.
>
> The introduction of a multitude of new craft and technician level courses over the last ten years has led to the engagement of an ever-increasing proportion of lower academically qualified and professionally untrained teachers ...
>
> Clearly as the future of further education colleges lies in meeting the needs of craft and

technician level work, the actions of the teachers in further education colleges are going to tend further towards those of the shop floor worker in industry. For those teachers who see their work as a career in a profession it would seem the time is opportune to form a professional body the objectives of which are (to depart from the trivial) to establish:

1. Basic entry qualifications into the profession.
2. A professional standard of conduct.
3. A united body incorporating all levels of education from nursery to university.
4. A progressive appraisal of educational needs accompanied by retraining programmes for teachers subject to implementing new courses.[54]

It was on the basis of such beliefs as these that soon after the Association of Polytechnic Teachers was formed in the polytechnics as an attempt at a breakaway from the ATTI.

The question of the closed shop was, however, overshadowed at the next Conference by an even larger issue, that of the Industrial Relations Bill. An Executive motion came top of the list of priority motions for Conference with the result that the Association was committed to outright opposition even before the Bill became law:

Conference affirms its opposition to the Industrial Relations Bill and instructs the Executive Committee:

a. to support the Trades Union Congress in its opposition to the Bill should it become law;
b. not to register or de-register as may be appropriate without the advice of the TUC and the approval of Council;
c. to pursue a policy of non-cooperation with any agencies set up under the Act;
d. to work for the repeal of the Act at the earliest opportunity.[55]

If, as Lockwood said, identification with the wider labour movement and action in concert 'in critical class situations' are important measures of class consciousness, then the

ATTI as a body had come a long way down that road by 1971. During the debate the Bill was described as 'nothing but a plan to shackle the unions'. When attempts were made to remove clauses (b) and (c) on the grounds that lecturers as responsible citizens should not be encouraging 'lawlessness', they were met with the strong ideological counterargument that 'if a law is passed which has taken away the fundamental rights of the trade union movement ... do we say it is not a sufficiently bad law to disregard it?'[56] Conference did not seem to think so and the amendment was lost.

THE HOUGHTON AWARD
There was a Labour Government in power and an ex-teacher, Edward Short, at the Department of Education when the teachers won their interim award in 1970 and it took them six months of campaigning, sanctions and strikes to get it. Within two years the teachers were on the move again, this time over an increase in the London allowance in the face of a Conservative-imposed incomes policy. This dispute is considered to be something of a milestone in Association history not only because it was the first time college lecturers took action on their own behalf, but also because the Executive actually instructed its members in London to take strike action. Consequently, in March 1973, 14 ATTI branches took part in three-day strikes organised alongside the NUT and there were strikes and demonstrations in other colleges on 21 March when the NUT had called out all its London teachers on a one-day strike. There was no immediate settlement, however, and the claim still lay on the table when a Labour Government took office in February 1974. Whilst committed to the repeal of the Conservative Party's Counter Inflation Act which had announced Phase 3 of its incomes policy in the previous December, the new Secretary of State for Education, Reg Prentice, asked the teachers to wait until the report of the Pay Board to which the matter had been referred. The London teachers replied with a massive lobby of Parliament on 29 April, coupled with the threat of mass resignations should the new government not agree to a substantial increase in the allowance. In Parliament that day, the two major political parties vied with each other to show sympathy for the London teachers. In his turn, Reg Prentice promised the teachers significant increases and urged them not to hand in their resignations as they had threatened so

shortly before the increases were due to be announced.

In the meantime, successive government incomes policies had eroded teachers' pay in both absolute and relative terms. In the eight years from 1965 to 1973, for example, lecturers' pay had risen in cash terms by 46.6 per cent, the Retail Price Index by 58 per cent. Average wages had risen by some 87.5 per cent over the same period and salaries by an even greater 96.5 per cent. Lecturers' pay compared badly with practically every reference group the Association cared to name. These salary problems were, however, temporarily resolved by the new Labour Government which set up an independent review body to look into the whole question of teachers' pay. That body, the Houghton Committee, reported in December 1974 and recommended average wage increases of 26 per cent, the abolition of the assistant lecturer scale and automatic progression from Lecturer II to Senior Lecturer for those engaged in advanced work. Houghton was a comparability study and the point of comparison was not the wage levels of manual workers but the salaries and career structures of other professions. 'Teaching,' the Committee said, 'is a profession ... Entry to the profession is the threshold of a career, which should provide both steady and secure employment for the diligent and qualified, and opportunities for promotion desirable and adequate for those who aspire to the highest positions.'[57]

There is no doubt that both the setting up of Houghton and the rapid implementation of its proposals were a product of the school teachers' sustained campaign over salaries during the whole period from 1969. Indeed this was the strong implication of an article in the educational press written by a member of the Burnham management panel immediately after the report was published. Challenging the teachers to 'respond positively' to Houghton, the writer claimed that the Committee had been set up in a 'crisis atmosphere' and strongly condemned the Scottish teachers who had carried out a general strike threat immediately prior to the Committee's report. Hoping that Houghton would 'bring peace in an area of public life which could give society the leadership it needs', he made an appeal to traditional professional values:

> Given adequate salaries, the colleges, polytechnics
> and schools might now resolutely seek to provide,
> as so many already do, some still point in the

turning world where educational values of ration-
ality and concern for other people and social
cohesion can find their strongholds. In the colleges
and the schools, there could now be a decisive
move by the teaching profession to combat the
yelling and the striking and the bullying that is
becoming all too prevalent.[58]

In fact, the teachers did not accept Houghton gratefully.
The first meeting of the Burnham Technical Committee
after the report was picketed by ATTI members to ensure
its early implementation. As a result of such pressure, the
teachers gained an interim payment because, we are told,
'of the hysterical and condescending assumptions that
teachers could not wait an extra month for their money and
it would keep the wild men quiet'.[59] It was ironic indeed
that the teachers had at last gained official recognition of
their status as professionals through militant trade union-
like action.

NOTES

1. Kenneth Prandy, <u>Professional Employees</u> (Faber,
1965).
2. Thus, in 1945 the basic scale for qualified assistant
teachers recommended by the Burnham Main Committee
was that recommended by the Technical Committee for
Assistant Lecturers Grade A. Training and graduate
allowances were the same although special responsibility
allowances were paid to up to 20 per cent of assistants in
the colleges as opposed to 15 per cent in the schools. For
further details of salary structure during these years see
<u>The First Half Century</u>, ATTI, 1955.
3. Another major step forward for the profession
embodied in this report was the assimilation of the
instructor grade into the basic scale. This was seen as an
important step in raising the status of the craft teacher and
as such the status of the profession as a whole.
4. <u>Technical Journal</u>, June 1945.
5. Ibid. June 1948.
6. Ibid. June 1951.
7. Correspondence in <u>The Times Educational
Supplement</u>, 12 March 1954.
8. Ibid. 4 June 1954.
9. Ibid.

10. Ibid. 21 May 1954.
11. Reported in the Executive Committee Minutes, 1954.
12. Technical Journal, May 1955.
13. See R.D. Coates, Teachers' Unions and Interest Group Politics, (Cambridge University Press, 1972) and R.A. Manzer, Teachers and Politics: The Role of the NUT in the Making of National Education Policy in England and Wales since 1944 (Manchester University Press, 1970) for details of this dispute.
14. Executive Minutes, 1952.
15. Technical Journal, July 1963.
16. Ibid. July 1959.
17. Ibid. Feb. 1965.
18. 'Report of Special Conference', Council Minutes, 1966.
19. G. Routh, 'White-Collar Unions in the United Kingdom' in Adolf Sturmthal (ed), White-Collar Trade Unions (University of Illinois, 1966), p.165.
20. A.J.H. Sykes, 'Some Differences in the Attitudes of Clerical and of Manual Workers', Sociological Review, XIII, November 1965, p.117.
21. Prandy, Professional Employees, p.37.
22. George Strauss, 'White-Collar Unions are Different', Harvard Business Review, XXXII, 1954, pp.73-82.
23. David Lockwood, The Blackcoated Worker (Allen & Unwin, 1958), p.137.
24. See G.S. Bain et al., Social Stratification and Trade Unionism (Heinemann, 1973) where the authors summarise the literature on trade unionism and social imagery in terms of these two basic dichotomies.
25. Lockwood, The Blackcoated Worker, p.137.
26. Ibid. pp.137-8.
27. R.M. Blackburn, Union Character and Social Class (Batsford, 1967).
28. Routh, 'White-Collar Unions in the United Kingdom', p.202.
29. Bain et al., Social Stratification, p.92.
30. Ibid. p.90.
31. C. Wright Mills, White Collar (Oxford University Press, 1951), pp.308-9.
32. Coates, Teachers' Unions, p.127.
33. 'Report of Special Conference on TUC Affiliation', Technical Journal, October 1966.
34. Ibid. July 1965.

35. 'Report of Special Conference', October 1966.
36. Ibid.
37. Technical Journal, October 1963.
38. Ibid.
39. Ibid. February 1966. This letter in its turn brought forward strong opposition along the lines that the government had every right to interfere as, in the end, it footed the bill; that trade union power was in fact the cause of Britain's ills and that trade union reform would be more likely to bring teachers a higher salary and status than 'well-tried trade union methods'.
40. Blackburn, Union Character, p.37.
41. Council Minutes, 1967.
42. Technical Journal, February 1968. Whilst the NUT campaign of 1967 did indeed result in significant gains for the school teachers, they were not in terms of the salary claim originally put forward. The original goal had been a sigificant increase on the basic scale and an end to the primary/secondary differential. In the settlement, the employers committed themselves only to a reduction of differentials at some point in the future. Nothing was done on the basic scale. What the school teachers did gain, however, was a working party to look into how best to end compulsory school meal supervision and the question of the unqualified teachers.
43. Ibid. November 1969.
44. Ibid. December 1969. See V. Burke, Teachers in Turmoil (Penguin 1971) for a full and sympathetic acount of the teachers' action.
45. The Technical Journal, January 1970. In this issue of the Technical Journal, the Executive saw fit to publish reports of the success of various local actions, behind which, the Journal states 'is a story of enterprise by the branches, increased commitment and solidarity among members, and growth in membership'. Whilst these successes were, of course, not the whole story, their publication marks the transition of the Technical Journal into a journal campaigning for action and as such represents a significant departure from the former 'professional' image they sought to project.
46. Ibid. March 1970.
47. Ibid. October 1969.
48. Ibid. December 1969.
49. Quoted in Burke, Teachers in Turmoil, pp.48-9.
50. Technical Journal, June 1969. None of the

prominent members of the Association interviewed by the writer in the early seventies saw the Teachers' Council has having any relevance to the problems of the profession. Indeed, the General Secretary of the NUT at the time (and past General Secretary of the ATTI) summed up the general feeling quite nicely when he said, 'What's the point in having a Teaching Council in which you pay £2 in order to discipline yourself more harshly than somebody disciplines you at the moment for nothing?'

51. Fieldwork, Spring, 1973/4.
52. Technical Journal, July 1970.
53. Ibid.
54. The Times Educational Supplement, 5 July 1970.
55. Technical Journal, June 1971.
56. Ibid.
57. For a summary of these and the other principle recommendations embodied in the report see The Times Higher Education Supplement, 'Houghton Special Supplement', 27 December 1974. One of the most significant recommendations as they affected college lecturers was the recognition of parity between teachers of advanced work in the colleges and lecturers in the universities. This must have come as some relief to the ATTI given the relative disadvantage polytechnic lecturers had suffered after a succession of flat-rate awards under incomes policy which provided the basis for the Association of Polytechnic Teachers, founded in ideological opposition to the trade union principles avowed by the ATTI to recruit in the polytechnics.
58. Maurice Kogan, 'Teachers Challenged to Respond Positively', ibid. p.4.
59. Ibid.

PART THREE

THE LIMITS TO COLLECTIVE CONTROL

5

On The College Floor

ALL TRADE UNIONISTS NOW?

It has been argued that the growing 'unionateness' of the ATTI represented no mere mechanical adaptation to changes in its environment but a significant change in character from a status-conscious professional association to a class-conscious trade union. Indeed it is verging on truism to argue that one can explain the increasingly union-like character of the teachers' associations over the period in question in terms of an adaptation to their declining influence in the 'educational sub-government' and the stringent application of government incomes policy. Of course it was! Even the industrial working class were not born trade unionists but had to learn the necessity for trade unionism through their dealings with intransigent employers. What is of more theoretical significance is that given changes in its environment, there took place within the Association an ideological struggle as to what should be the mode of adaptation. Should it become more like a trade union or not? Faced with an equally hostile environment earlier in its history (in 1954, for example) the answer had been no. Earlier still, the question had not even been considered. We cannot, therefore, agree with Bain when he argues, that 'union behaviour is often not so much determined by the attitudes of union members as by structural factors external to them'.[1] In the case of the ATTI, it was not only the environment which had changed but attitudes and values amongst its members.

This was quite apparent to those amongst the leadership of the Association during the transitional period, both old-guard and new. All those interviewed were in agreement that the Association had become more union-like in character and all suggested the same environmental factors (incomes policy and ministerial intervention in Burnham negotiations) as the context in which this had taken place. But when asked to explain why the Association had responded in the way it did, all equally referred to the changing composition and orientations of the membership. For example, one past General Secretary, a committed trade unionist, placed great emphasis on the expansion which had taken place in the profession, especially in the numbers of people from industry at below technologist level 'where trade unionism already had a grip':

> We've always had these people, but they used to be the good boys, the ones who had made it from the shop floor. Now we are recruiting people who are more trade-union conscious than traditionally that element was ... It was once the professional engineer who dominated the Association, amongst some of the most right-wing people in the country. Technologists are not generally the most progressive of people either educationally or politically. But over time we've recruited more from the strata just below that. Trade unionism is not a bogey to them.[2]

A past-president of the Association, another committed trade unionist, agreed with this analysis of the old-style teacher from industry who 'had come up the hard way' and 'was narrowly vocational in outlook and individualistic in motivation'. 'They had no background of being in a trade union,' he explained, 'their courses were narrowly vocational and they saw their role as passing on their skills and their type of motivation. This did not include any collective values.'

Another past-president, this time a member of the old-guard, placed special emphasis on the influx of craft rather than technician level teachers into the profession. 'Trade unionism', he thought, 'was coming from the colleges doing lower-level work. Not the professionals in colleges like mine where there's still sufficient of the old professional attitude left to make them unhappy about putting their own personal interests first.' An influx of graduates straight from university was also agreed to be a contributing factor, especially the social scientists on the more socially-oriented courses. Indeed, the general consensus might best be summed up in the words of yet another past-president, a self-styled 'professional' who had been pushed into a more militant attitude by the events in question:

The whole structure of the profession tends to

make us more left-wing. We are made up more and
more of workers and social studies graduates. The
background of these people tends to be more left-
wing than right-wing. Also the youth in the
Association ... and it is the youth who are feeling
the pinch. You see the earlier membership liked to
think of themselves as professional gentlemen.
They didn't like associating with the workers they
had stopped being themselves. I've noticed that
people who have come up the hard way react the
most strongly against their former colleagues: 'I
have now gone beyond the working class, I don't
want to know anything about trade unionism.'[3]

The implication was that by the 1970s, the base for trade
unionism was sufficiently broad to make union-like
behaviour a realistic possibility.

What remains problematic, however, is the extent to
which the increasingly class-conscious policies of the
Association were shared by the membership as a whole. As
Bain put it in his critique of the concept of 'unionateness',
even granted that its measures did provide an accurate and
unambiguous measure of class consciousness (which we have
argued they did in the case of the ATTI) then:

it is debateable whose class-consciousness they
measure. To assume that they measure the class-
consciousness of members is to ignore the political
process within unions and to overstate the degree
to which the attitudes of the leadership can be
used as a guide to those of the membership.
Although membership attitudes are no doubt a
constraint on leadership behaviour, there is
abundant evidence to indicate the lack of
congruence between the two.[4]

Lockwood himself was not unaware of this problem in his
survey of early clerical unionism where 'in some cases, the
leadership has proved to be less radical in its outlook ... than
the mass membership; in others the relationship has been
the reverse.'[5] It was generally agreed that exactly the same
could be said of the ATTI: once it had been a question of the
membership pushing the old-style leadership into more
unionate policies; now there was the difficulty of just how
far you could pull the membership with you, the political

127

process within the ATTI being such that decisions were made by the activists within the Association and, in the words of one full-time officer, 'activists do on occasion take decisions the majority would not agree with'.

Indeed, some amongst the old-guard in the Association went as far as to say that the more union-like policies of the ATTI bore no relationship to the membership at all and that decisions were pushed through by a minority of politically motivated activists in an undemocratic way. The trade unionists replied that the conditions for union democracy exist and should the membership disagree with policy they have the power to change it. But whilst it is of course true that the conditions for union democracy exist, otherwise how else could the trade unionists themselves have come to power in the Association, there is evidence to suggest that the average union member takes little interest in the broader affairs of the union, still less participates actively in decision-making. Whilst this is probably no less true of the ATTI than any other union, the point must be made that its 'progress leftwards' brought very little concrete opposition. There were few resignations after TUC affiliation and the strikes at the end of the decade brought record increases in membership. It would also be difficult to argue that the Association's character, at this time, was keeping potential members out since the level of 'completeness' was higher in the early seventies than it had ever been. On the other hand, from our knowledge of the attitudes and values of the early membership, one is inclined to believe the President of 1907 when he stated that should the Association become a technical teachers' trade union, it would very definitely break up. This was far from happening in the late sixties and early seventies.

Those who have sought to challenge the relationship between unionisation and consciousness of class, especially amongst white-collar employees, would argue that this might well be because the social meaning of trade unionism has itself changed significantly over recent years. Having become 'institutionalised', it has become devoid of the class connotations it once had. Similar in intent are those arguments which stress the white-collar workers' instrumental attachment to his union, it being seen, in the words of C. Wright Mills, as 'something to be used, rather than as something in which to believe'.[6] Given an instrumental attachment to the union it is quite possible that the individual member might see its class-conscious policies as merely something which unions do and which they are prepared to tolerate as long as they are not directly affected. Roberts strongly implies that this was the case amongst the fast growing technicians' unions in the sixties:

> The history of technicians' unions suggests that this category of worker is strongly status-conscious, but status is seen in strictly labour market terms. Professional associations that are concerned mainly with non-pecuniary aspects of status do not fully satisfy the strong desires of technicians for higher relative levels of remuneration. On the other hand, appeals to class concepts of trade unionism make little impact. Although the leadership of these unions has tended to be committed to left-wing Socialism, and even Communism, the collective bargaining policy actually adopted has reflected the practical requirements of the membership. The ideological wish of the leadership to attack the capitalist system, and the interest of members in securing immediate tangible monetary gains, have come together in a mutually satisfying aggressive policy to secure higher pay and improved conditions of employment.[7]

And Carter's more recent work on ASTMS, for example, has reinforced the point.[8]

In an effort to assess the strength of their commitment to trade unionism once the ATTI's transition to a more 'unionate' body had been made, college lecturers were asked which of a series of statements came nearest to their views on trade unionism for teachers (Table 5.1). Those who responded positively to the first item were thought to be the remaining 'harmonistic collectivists' within the Association. Whilst recognising that a collective strategy was appropriate in their situation, there was no positive commitment to the trade union ideal. Those preferring the second item, on the other hand, did see the necessity for trade unionism for teachers even if they were not totally happy about it. Those responding positively to the fourth item did not even see the need for collective representation. Here the union was seen in the purely individualistic terms of providing personal insurance should something go wrong at work. On this count 26 per cent of the lecturers could not be called trade unionists at all, whilst a further 24 per cent were reluctant in their allegiance. This leaves almost half of the sample showing something like a positive commitment to the idea of trade unionism for teachers.

Table 5.1: The need for trade unionism for teachers

	% agree
Teachers need an organisation to talk over their problems with employers, though this need not necessarily be a trade union	17
A trade union is not the ideal way of protecting the interests of professional people like teachers but unfortunately in public employment it is necessary	24
A trade union is the only way teachers can protect their interests effectively	48
Teachers need an organisation like the ATTI primarily to provide legal assistance to its members	9
No information	1
	(100)
	(N = 457)

Source: survey data

These different degrees of commitment to the principle of trade unonism for teachers were mirrored in the reasons given for joining the ATTI. Many of those who thought a trade union was the only way to protect teachers' interests said they had joined because in some way they 'believed in' trade unionism and talked in terms of variants on the old trade-union principle of 'unity is strength'. Not so the more reluctant trade unionists who quite often articulated the need for union representation in terms of the need for individual protection under bureaucratic conditions:

I joined because I am not in sole charge of my own salary and conditions of service. I no longer decide whether I can accept a job on the terms offered.
> Senior Lecturer, aged 45, Management Studies

You need protection in a large organisation.
> Lecturer II, aged 33, Social Studies

I felt I might need the backing of the union in disputes with my employers if any personal ones arose.
> Senior Lecturer, aged 51, Mechanical Engineering

Others talked in terms of payment in kind for services rendered:

As the union gets pay increases, it is obviously wrong to do anything other than join.
> Senior Lecturer, aged 53, Electrical Engineering

Non-members want to take the benefits without paying. That is not fair play.
> Principal Lecturer, aged 47, Management Studies

Whilst such responses might seem to indicate a normative dimension, it would be wrong to assume that it was necessarily collectivist in content. 'What I pay the ATTI as a professional association,' said one member with a highly individualistic orientation, 'is what you might pay a solicitor to get you a higher salary.'

As might be expected, therefore, a not insignificant minority of college lecturers (22 per cent) still objected to TUC affiliation. Their greatest single worry was that the TUC was a party political body, but most of those opposed to affiliation also believed that the ATTI was not really a trade union and affiliation on that basis was not therefore appropriate. By way of contrast, the greatest single source of agreement in favour of TUC affiliation (63 per cent) was with the statement that the ATTI was a trade union and as a trade union it needed a wider voice and platform. Some 56 per cent of the sample agreed that the ATTI should be affiliated because the government consulted with the TUC on matters of economic policy which greatly affected teachers and only 20 per cent believed that a major reason for affiliation ought to be the TUC's concern with education

131

and training. But what was perhaps most significant about the pattern of response was the large proportion of college lecturers (almost 40 per cent) who admitted to having no strong feelings either way on the question, irony indeed given the passion with which the debate had been conducted less than a decade earlier. By the seventies, it would seem that trade unionism was no longer the bogey it had once been amongst college lecturers. Government incomes policies had highlighted the structurally weak position of public employees, whether white-collar or blue, and white-collar workers generally were more organised than ever before. Under such circumstances the traditional siren cry of professionalism as opposed to trade unionism now lacked credibility and in a very real sense the college lecturers, like other white-collar workers, were 'all trade unionists now'.

It would seem that by the seventies, the terms of the ideological debate were already shifting away from the false dichotomy between professionalism and trade unionism and into the arena of 'moderate' vs 'militant' trade unionism. It is necessary to ask, therefore, how far a commitment to the need for trade unionism for teachers necessarily involved a commitment to the use of 'all forms of industrial action which may be effective'. When asked whether they were happy about the use of sanctions to further their interests, 35 per cent of the lecturers replied that they were, some 40 per cent were not and a further 20 per cent were really not sure. As might have been expected, there was a strong correlation between those who were positively committed to the idea of trade unionism for teachers and the willingness to embrace sanctions, but what was most interesting was that almost half of the committed trade unionists were not happy with the idea of sanctions. This less than perfect correlation can at least in part be explained by worries as to their effectiveness given the purely 'voluntary' nature of much public sector further and higher education:

> In principle, I've got no objection to teachers going out on strike. We're just like any other workers. But, unfortunately, they're rather ineffectual. The employers don't lose money, they save it. They're laughing all the way to the bank.

> We've got even less power than the school teachers. When they go on strike, the mums have

to stay off work and there's soon a rumpus. If we went on strike, nobody would notice. The employers would be glad to get the kids back at work for the day.

All a strike in FE would do would be to harm the students, which seems a bit pointless.

The concern which many college lecturers felt about their lack of industrial muscle was best summed up by one branch secretary who explained that:

Many times at branch meetings people have taken the view that the only action we could take would put money into the coffers rather than take it out ... And anything which brings into disrepute the role of our college in the community is a bad thing. Local concerns, industry, won't look at it sympathetically ... they'll just look at the inconvenience it's causing them and they might not send their students here again.

Given the competition for students and courses which many colleges might find themselves in, this could be a very serious threat indeed.

However, not all those who were unhappy about the use of sanctions were unhappy for purely pragmatic reasons. For example, whilst only a quarter of the lecturers believed that 'give and take' would get them very far in negotiations (thus indicating the majority did not feel that the employers were exactly on their side) not all were willing to follow this through to its logical conclusion. Many preferred to believe instead in the value of greater skill in negotiation and more expertise in the calculation and presentation of claims. During the fieldwork, it was quite common to hear lecturers make very militant sounding noises about the need for a trade union and then go on to deny the need for sanctions. One teacher of management studies, for example, who described himself as 'an old-style socialist', said he believed wholeheartedly in the need for a trade union for teachers:

You need a union in teaching as much as in industry. There's a latent medievalism in teaching. I remember how my mother (she was a teacher) used to have to go round knocking on the door of

> the doctor and the priest to get her salary. They'd
> do that now if there was no union. You've got to
> have class feeling. They don't even want teachers
> too well educated in case they get uppity. If the
> union didn't drive for better training and such
> things they would soon grind you down.

He was equally virulent about management in the colleges.
'The principals in some of these places,' he said, 'are like a
holy trinity unto themselves; some buggers in a position of
authority are no more than dictators.' And yet when asked
how he felt about taking strike action, he thought that the
issue would have to be very extreme indeed for him to
contemplate it. 'I teach management,' he said, 'and generally
it's failure on both parts to communicate.' Similarly a
younger teacher of radiography thought that 'employers are
no more sympathetic to professional workers than they are
to manual workers; employers are the same everywhere,
they always take advantage.' At the same time, he thought
that there was no need to be always 'battling it out'. What
lecturers needed was another Clive Jenkins, a good public
relations man who could present their case better to the
employers and to the public. Indeed, the attitude of this
group of lecturers can be best summed up in the words of a
teacher of industrial relations whose informed opinion as to
why the ATTI did not achieve its goals was that his granny
could negotiate better (but not, note, that she would go out
on strike!).

That such inconsistencies existed in the minds of many
college lecturers should not in itself be surprising. Many
writers have commented on the complex and contradictory
nature of consciousness of class and employment relations
on the part of manual workers and such workers have had a
much longer experience of conflict than have college
lecturers. Blackburn and Mann, for example, in their study
of unskilled workers in Peterborough argue that it is only
natural for workers to be 'confused'. Workers as well as
having interests in common:

> are also in touch with rival interpretations of their
> common reality. Through the mass media and
> workplace interaction, they learn that 'strikes are
> caused by agitators and extremists', that 'loyalty' is
> a much prized virtue but also that men should work
> for their living (and shareholders do not), and that

'management think only of profits'. There is only
one ideological sub-culture to which workers can
adhere, the working-class 'proletarian' ideology,
and very few are committed to it. Most remain
confused by the clash between conservatism and
proletarianism, but touched by both ...[9]

This confusion, they claim, stems from the contradictions
inherent in a capitalist economy characterised by 'co-
operation in pursuit of scarcity'. This, they argue:

may not take us very far towards a theory of
society, but it does enable us to make more sense
of workers' images. For instead of viewing them as
approximations to consistent and coherent images,
we should regard them as attempts to grapple with
the real contradictions of the workers' situation.[10]

On the other hand, recent writers within the neo-
Marxist tradition have insisted that the inconsistencies in
consciousness amongst white-collar workers stem not so
much from the contradictions inherent in a capitalist
economy as from the contradictions inherent in their class
position as members of 'the new middle class'. Located in a
structurally ambiguous position between capital and labour,
members of the new middle class engage in forms of
collective representation which reflect the ambiguity of
their objective class position. Thus, the traditional Marxist
ownership/non-ownership dichotomy is an inadequate
indicator of class location. Although some structuralists
would agree that white-collar unionism is the product of the
'proletarianisation' of white-collar workers under conditions
of advanced monopoly capitalism, this proletarianisation can
never be complete for as long as they retain any role within
the global function of capital. Others would go so far as to
argue that proletarianisation is not possible at all for as long
as changes in the work situation of white-collar workers
involve a mere loss of autonomy within the global functions
of capital rather than the replacement of capital by labour
functions. Concern over such issues as income differentials
and promotion prospects, or the reluctance to use the strike
weapon, are seen as indicative of this 'new middle class'
status and and white-collar unionism far from indicating a
proletarian consciousness, might even be reactionary in
content in so far as it pursues demands which run counter to

the interests of the 'real' working class.[11]

There are obvious problems with such an approach, not least that many of the indicators of new middle-class status are just as ambiguous as the indicators of 'unionateness' have been said to be. Ogza and Lawn, for example, in their critique of the various structuralist positions argue that:

> The precise nature of the relationship between political, ideological and the economic or technical determinants of class location ... has been either rendered obscure or has been reduced to a form which very nearly reproduces the work of non-Marxist class theoreticians, with its invocations of a mental/manual divide, its stress on supervisory functions and its use of vague criteria such as 'common lifestyle' to establish class identity.

To illustrate the point, one excellent attempt to ground structuralist theory in empirical analysis argues that a group of foremen in an East Midlands engineering works are new middle class given their role, however minimal in this particular instance, within the global functions of capital despite the fact that their strong craft identity and pride had once located them firmly as workers within the technical division of labour. Once members of the AUEW, now of TASS, the study argues that 'their behaviour in general and their trade unionism in particular was influenced by the fact that they were middle-class workers' and cites in support of this argument the fact that during an occupation against factory closure the foremen were concerned to preserve the machinery on their section in good order and to prevent its being stolen.[13] But what, it might be asked, is more indicative of class position, the foremen's concern to prevent theft and vandalism, or the fact that they were in the occupation at all? In the same volume, what is believed to be the increasingly less 'unionate' character of TASS is explained in terms of its more recent policy of recruiting managers and graduate engineers. Without wishing to commit the heresy of equating subjective consciousness with objective class position, there is a problem here in that both managers and graduate engineers are held to be responsible for the same set of policy changes, when, according to the writer at least, they occupy different class locations.

Similarly, it would be difficult to explain the different

orientations to trade unionism amongst the ATTI membership with reference to differences in their imputed structural class location. There was evidence from the survey data to suggest that the grade of a lecturer (which at the higher levels might be taken as an index of new middle-class status in that it is indicative of some form of control function) was not a strong indicator of ideological predisposition once the factors of age and subject taught had been controlled for. Indeed the leadership of the Association were proved right in their explanation of its change in character in terms of the influx of young graduates into the profession. For example, 65 per cent of those lecturers under the age of 30 and 55 per cent under the age of 35 believed that trade unionism was the only way teachers could protect their interests as opposed to some 28 per cent aged 55 and over, a pattern of response which was mirrored in their attitudes to TUC affiliation. Furthermore, the relationship between age and preparedness to use sanctions was even stronger than the relationship between age and more general trade union views. It was therefore to be expected that the younger the trade unionist, the less likely he or she would be to shy away from the use of sanctions. This did indeed turn out to be the case with over three-quarters of the teachers under the age of 30 who believed that trade unionism was the only way to protect teachers' interests also happy about the use of sanctions in pursuit of their interests, however those interests might be defined.

This figure was not dissimilar to the proportion of social scientists who were quite happy about the idea of using sanctions. Indeed, 76 per cent of social science teachers and 54 per cent of those in the arts and humanities were happy with sanctions as compared with only 27 per cent of teachers in business and management subjects and technology. Somewhere in between came the teachers of natural science and production and craft-level subjects with some 35 per cent happy about the use of sanctions. This distribution did in general terms match the distribution of age between the different subject groups. What was interesting, for example, was the relatively small proportion of teachers from the lower rungs of industry who were wholeheartedly committed to the idea of trade unionism for teachers, even though many of them had been members of manual trade unions in their past. It had been thought that those lecturers who had been members of a manual trade union in their previous occupations might be socialised into the norms and values of the trade union movement and might show a more positive understanding of the need for trade unionism and the use of sanctions than those who had not previously been members. In fact those who had been members of a manual trade union for more than five years were no more likely to be happy with trade unionism than those who had not been members at all. On the other hand, those who had been members of either a white-collar or manual trade union in their previous occupations for less than five years were much more likely to embrace militant trade unionism. The difference here is again the age factor. It is likely that the lack of trade-union consciousness on the part of those who had been members of a manual union for some time previously can be explained by the fact that they had crossed the manual/non-manual divide in industry at a time when the status distinctions between staff and line were greater than today and when white-collar unionism had less of a grip. Like the original technical teachers, they were concerned to assert their new-found status and far from embracing the norms and values of trade unionism, this quite obviously involved a rejection of them.

However, the point stands that there was some relationship between the policies of the union and the orientations of its members. In the case of the ATTI, far from its policies telling us nothing about the consciousness of its members, it was a change in their consciousness (consequent in part upon a change in their composition) which brought about changes in organisational behaviour. Even if, in the mass, this change in consciousness had only entailed a change in the definition of how best to pursue individual or group, as opposed to class, interest, this would not have meant that it was totally devoid of ideological content. The very recognition that interests cannot be protected individually and further that collective action in the form of a trade union might be necessary to successfully pursue them represents a very different consciousness from that of the old-style professional. On the other hand, it is quite clear from the above considerations that membership of a trade union (however 'unionate') does not <u>necessarily</u> entail a consciousness of class (however primitive) on the part of the individual member and this is true of both white-collar and manual unions. Indeed, as Price argues in his summary of the literature on white-collar unionism, rather than assume an 'easy equation between union membership and the adoption of a general collectivist philosophy', a more useful approach to the understanding of trade union character might well be 'to assess the issues on which a collectivist strategy is to be held appropriate, and those on which individual strategies are seen as valid'.[14] That there were structural as well as ideological limitations placed on the availability and effectiveness of collective strategies for college lecturers has already been established. We shall see that given the nature of their work there were also issues where lecturers might positively prefer an individual rather than a collective response, independent of either pragmatic or ideological considerations.

A FAIR RATE FOR THE JOB

It has been argued that professionalism as an occupational strategy was inappropriate for technical teachers because of their essential status as employees. Although professionals in the sense that their occupational role involved the application of specialist expertise and knowledge, they were not independent professionals providing a service to clients but were dependent on an employer more powerful than themselves for both their livelihood and the opportunity to put their knowledge and skills into practice. As such their adherence to the professional ideal had no concrete expression in reality but rather articulated an ideological stance which has been defined as status-consciousness. Status-consciousness in this sense refers to a particular world-view, the kernel of which is an understanding of social relations in general and employment relations in particular in terms of a unity rather than a conflict of interest. It cannot be equated with either the maintenance of salary differentials or the concern over promotion prospects which have often been taken as indices of such consciousness. That concern over salary differentials and promotion prospects are not necessarily equatable with a such a world-view can be seen from the college lecturers' attitude to both their salaries and salary structure in the years immediately prior to the Houghton Report when material concerns were uppermost in the teachers' minds.

Over two-thirds of the lecturers asked were positively dissatisfied with their salary, a pattern of response which was not, perhaps, surprising given that Houghton itself was designed to rectify the extent to which teachers' salaries had fallen behind in both absolute and relative terms. What is of more interest is the type of reason the lecturers gave to explain their dissatisfaction. The ways in which writers have often dismissed the symbolic significance of white-collar trade unionism have already been discussed, the general gist of their arguments being that for white-collar workers the union is merely something to be used rather than in which to believe and, moreover, to be used to maintain traditional differentials and hence social distance between manual and non-manual occupations. White-collar unions are the embodiment of status, not class, consciousness. But concern over narrowing differentials between themselves and manual workers did not seem to be of major importance where the lecturers' attitudes to their salaries were at issue. Rather, their major source of dissatisfaction was that given either their qualifications, experience or felt abilities they could be earning more elsewhere, either in industry or in other professions. In other words, the salient reference group here was workers with marketable skills similar to their own, a positive reference group, not the negative one of a lower-status group 'catching up'.

In fact, when the criteria lecturers used to assess their salaries were examined in greater depth, it was apparent that they were expressing a judgement as to whether their salary was fair in relation to criteria which barely made reference to the earnings of manual workers and which differed little in kind from those used by other workers, whether white-collar or blue. Many writers on industrial relations have suggested that a significant component of any claim for more money is the normative element of 'fairness'. Hyman and Brough, for example, argue that 'the arguments of those involved in industrial relations are shot through with essentially moral terminology' and go on to distinguish between two analytically distinct sets of criteria or frames of reference which are used to judge whether income is 'fair' or not. The first, which they term 'internal' criteria, relates to the assessment of the pay of an individual or group by reference to the contributions made or capacities required in respect of such characteristics of the job as effort, qualification and aptitude. This frame of reference might best be summed up by the maxim 'a fair rate for the job'. The second set of criteria, which Hyman and Brough call 'external' criteria, relates to the assessment of pay by comparison with the income of other individuals or groups. This they call 'fair comparisons'. Whilst analytically distinct, the two frames of reference are not independent of each other in reality, internal criteria implicitly involving a judgement about the relative in-put of other workers in relation to their reward, albeit that that judgement is made within the limited reference group of other workers in the plant on similar jobs. Similarly, whilst external criteria involve explicit comparisons with broad occupational groups outside the worker's immediate experience, there is implicit comparison with the in-put of those other groups in terms of internal criteria.[15]

It has been found that manual workers tend to use internal criteria to judge income, white-collar and professional workers external criteria. This has been explained in terms of the restricted reference groups of the manual workers, restricted because knowledge of the income and in-put of occupational groups other than those with whom they come into immediate contact is limited and because skills tend to be non-transferable or specific to particular employment situations, thus making external comparisons difficult. But whether workers use internal criteria explicitly in terms of 'a fair rate for the job' or implicitly in terms of 'fair comparisons', those elements of the job which are deemed to be worthy of reward tend to be precisely those factors which characterise the worker's own occupation. Summarising empirical data on subjective job-evaluation, Hyman and Brough tell us that 'in evaluating pay, manual workers tended to refer to hard or unpleasant features connected with the work situation, whereas non-manual workers were more likely to mention responsibility, education or training'.[16]

The single most importance source of dissatisfaction with pay amongst college lecturers in the early seventies was that it had fallen behind in relation to the cost of living. The second most important source involved the principle of 'fair comparisons', though not, as many have suggested, with manual workers but with what they themselves might earn in industry or in the other professions. This is hardly surprising given that workers with some transferability of skills have been found to use predominantly external criteria when judging their salaries. The majority of college lecturers had had direct experience of these other fields of work and indeed might well be more qualified to practice them than some they had left behind. As far as college lecturers were concerned, Hyman's maxim 'familiarity breeds pay comparisons' is particularly apposite. Their dissatisfaction over pay seemed to represent genuine feelings of relative deprivation rather than mere rationalisations designed to legitimate the maintenance of differentials over and against manual workers:

> I honestly do not think it commensurate with the
> responsibility, work-load, expertise demanded of
> me, qualifications etc., if compared with other so-
> called professions where entry qualifications are
> similar, work load probably lighter and social use-
> fulness less obvious.
>> Senior Lecturer, aged 36, Polytechnic

> It is between £1000-£2000 p.a. below that for the
> sort of job I might be doing in industry and £1000
> below that of similar people in the universities.
>> Senior Lecturer, aged 40, Polytechnic

> After years of sacrifice getting more qualifica-
> tions, I still can't manage.
>> Lecturer II, aged 33, Physics

and those satisfied with their salaries used similar criteria:

> I think it is a fair salary compared with the
> equivalent job in industry. It seems about right for
> my abilities, responsibilities and work load.
>> Senior Lecturer, aged 35, Telecommunications

> Better than I'd get in industry, or school teaching
> or the Civil Service at my age.
>> Lecturer I, aged 23, Chemistry & Physics

> It is a fair salary for the amount of work I do,
> compared with the extra hours and pressure of
> work for about the same remuneration in industry.
>> Lecturer I, aged 35, Production Engineering

These responses indicate the extent to which the principle
of 'fair comparisons' does indeed involve the use of both
external and internal criteria. The lecturers judged the
fairness of other salaries not only on the basis of what
others with similar qualifications and experience earned but
also in relation to the relative 'in-puts' of the jobs they did.

Nevertheless, it did seem that in the delicate weighing
up process between the two, external criteria in general had
slightly more weight. This was particularly well illustrated
in the responses of those lecturers who were not really sure

what they felt about their salaries:

> I receive much less than equivalent staff in other
> organisations and there are such small differential
> bands between the Burnham grades. In absolute
> terms I think I really do not do at all badly and that
> others are effectively overpaid.
>
> Head of Department, aged 55

> It is at a level where I can live comfortably
> without being extravagant but compared with other
> people with my qualifications and experience I am
> £1000 below their salary. Against this I weigh job
> satisfaction.
>
> Senior Lecturer, aged 49, Accountancy

> I earn more than many who have less desirable jobs
> and much more than some over-worked school
> teachers, but I earn much less than university
> staffs although doing fairly similar work and less
> than some fairly lazy Poly staff, too. So I don't
> know.
>
> Senior Lecturer, aged 30, Polytechnic

So despite the fact that these lecturers felt that their
salaries were adequate for their needs, that they were both
conscious of others far less well off than themselves and
aware that their work offered a good deal of intrinsic job
satisfaction, the knowledge that others with similar
qualifications doing similar jobs were earning more
generated sufficient feelings of relative deprivation for
them to register less than complete satisfaction with their
pay.

In this context, the term status-consciousness is too
imprecise and value-laden a term to describe the criteria
lecturers used to judge the adequacy of their pay. At a time
when lecturers had fallen significantly behind in the wages
league, they were not comparing their salaries with those of
the manual working class and dissatisfied because their
differentials were being eroded. Rather they were assessing
the adequacy of their salaries against the market value of
their skills and that market value was inevitably judged in
terms of what others in the labour market were getting for
them. That in broad terms the market value of those skills
might embody the traditional status differentials between

143

manual and non-manual workers does not detract from the fact that most lecturers did not articulate their grievances in terms of wanting to maintain those differentials. On the contrary, their use of the principle of 'fair comparisons' differed little from that of other workers with some transferability of skill and that includes manual as well as white-collar and professional workers.

Similar arguments can be made about the lecturers' concern over promotion prospects. Almost two-thirds of the lecturers in the pre-Houghton survey were dissatisfied with their current grade in college and this contrasted sharply with the much smaller proportion (21 per cent) who said that opportunities for promotion were an important factor in deciding to take up lecturing in the first place. The reason for this apparent inconsistency lies in the lecturers' actual experience of the contradictions inherent in the grading system in the colleges. The establishment of a college determines the proportion of posts at different grades and is itself determined by a complex formula which takes into account both the size of a college in terms of student numbers and the levels of work taught. The establishment of an individual department within a college is determined by similar criteria. The grade of individual lecturers within this scheme would be determined by the number of posts at different grades available, the level of work they teach and the amount of administrative responsibility they undertake. For example, the Lecturer I scale is generally the grade at which teachers of non-advanced work would be appointed. Their promotion to Lecturer II would depend upon the amount of administrative responsibility undertaken and the availability of such a post in the department. Where establishment was blocked, the only way to achieve promotion would be to expand by putting on new courses thereby increasing the number of students. Only rarely would a teacher of non-advanced work become a Senior Lecturer, these posts occurring in any numbers only where a department teaching non-advanced work was exceptionally large. On the other hand, a teacher of advanced-level work, even with little experience, would be appointed at Lecturer II, and promotion to Senior Lecturer virtually guaranteed. To become a Principal Lecturer, however, would again depend upon the availability of such posts and the amount of administrative work undertaken. In the case of both teachers of advanced and non-advanced work, promotion to a higher grade would mean more administrative responsibility and less class contact.

Such a system of grading is riddled with contradictions. Where both advanced and non-advanced work is concerned, junior grades have a heavier teaching load than those with greater experience. In effect, the more actual teaching a college lecturer does, the less the pay and status in relation to other colleagues. Furthermore, the system whereby establishment is fixed according to some externally imposed formula might result in two lecturers doing exactly the same work but on different grades. This could of course happen within the same department where establishment is blocked. It might also happen with staff in different departments where one is rapidly expanding and the other not. In the same way, similarly qualified staff might be teaching different levels of work. For example, one physics graduate might be teaching at degree level, another at 'O' and 'A' level. The former would most likely be on a higher grade, teach less hours and be paid more money than the latter. Finally the very fact that pay and opportunities for promotion depend so much on level of work taught, rather than the actual job of teaching, might be resented by teachers of non-advanced work whose 'in-put' on many criteria might be considered just as high, if not higher, than many teachers of advanced-level work.

In short, with such a system of grading there was plenty of opportunity for the lecturers' sense of natural justice to be offended, this time by comparison with their own colleagues rather than with outside reference groups:

> Work of a comparable nature to mine is being done
> by others in college on a higher grade.
> > Lecturer I, aged 31, Biology

> I contribute as much or more than Senior Lecturers
> or Principal Lecturers but have no promotion
> prospects in the short term.
> > Lecturer, aged 26, Polytechnic

> I am as, or more, competent than many colleagues
> on higher grades. I do not get the 'rate for the job'.
> > Lecturer I, aged 27, Social Studies

And as with salaries, the qualities which lecturers put forward as worthy of reward tended to be their own:

I do more for my Lecturer II than others and the
Senior Lectureship was given to a craft teacher for
long service.
> Lecturer II, aged 52, Building Trades

I have better academic qualifications than at least
35 of the staff in my department.
> Lecturer II, aged 27, Polytechnic

Experience is underrated as against paper qualifications.
> Lecturer I, aged 44, English & Liberal Studies

and a young liberal studies teacher spoke for many when he
said:

I just cannot understand why grades should be
related to level of work taught. We all do the same
job - teaching.

Given the heterogeneity of the profession, the tendency
to make such judgements would be divisive enough without
further structural anomalies which gave rise to conflict and
resentment. Given the fixed number of senior posts at any
given time, many lecturers would be effectively debarred
from promotion not because of any lack of personal qualities
but because they were in the wrong place at the wrong time.
One Senior Lecturer summed up the general situation well:

It is very difficult to relate the justice of grades
and pay scales imposed from outside and by people
who have no conception of the actual work done.
Rigid establishment schemes lead to bitter and
unnecessary conflict and dissatisfaction between
departments and with those who have to operate
them.

And the inequitable grading of departments within the same
college did indeed cause considerable resentment:

Despite continuous and dedicated hard work at a
high level and endeavouring to keep pace with the
changing demands of both the students and the
selection bodies and maintaining an above average
record of student success, I have remained at my

present grade for ten years because of departmental grading while others in expanding departments have had advancement willy-nilly.

Lecturer II, aged 46, Art & Design

Because the Department is Grade 2, I do the job of
a Senior Lecturer but cannot get paid for it. I
regret changing departments from Engineering
which is the golden department.

Lecturer II, aged 41, Mathematics

Being in a small department we have no LIIs! I feel
after 28 years conscientious service I deserve an
LII. If I'd been in Engineering, I would have got it
years ago!

Lecturer I, aged 60, Woodwork

It is interesting to note that dissatisfaction with the system
of grades pre-dated the contraction of the next decade when
individual institutions were cut back, merged or even closed.
Even then, staff did not feel that grade was a true measure
of individual worth either to the college or, more especially,
to the students. Already able new recruits, and others
patiently biding their time, were finding promotion
prospects blocked by colleagues who had quite often
literally shot up the scales during the era of expansion, thus
increasing their feelings of relative deprivation. But such
feelings cannot be entirely explained with reference to
blocked career prospects alone. Dissatisfaction was too
widespread and deeply felt for that. Rather, the legitimacy
of the imputed criteria for promotion was widely questioned
and hence strong normative elements of natural justice were
involved. College lecturers were comparing the jobs they
did with the 'in-puts' of certain of their colleagues and once
again this made lecturers feel that they were not getting 'a
fair rate for the job'.[17]

Concern over promotion has often been taken as
evidence of middle class individualism and status-consciousness by many observers of white-collar and professional
employees. On this basis, for example, Roberts concludes
from his study of technicians that 'this category of worker is
strongly status-conscious'. He then uses this 'status-
consciousness' as an explanation as to why 'appeals to class
concepts of trade unionism (amongst technicians) make
little impact'.[18] Blalock, on the other hand, found that high

147

job aspirations amongst a group of undergraduates he studied did not correlate at all with other such indices of status-consciousness as social distancing behaviour, respect for status and patterns of conspicuous consumption. Finding also that 'persons with high job aspirations tended to have relatively less respect for status than those with lower job aspirations', he suggests that high job aspirations are relatively independent of the other indices of status-consciousness and indeed might not be a measure of it at all![19] Without wishing to deny the divisive nature of any payment system which emphasises individual rather than collective advancement, it seems clear from many of the lecturers' attitudes to promotion within the colleges that concern over promotion prospects cannot always be explained away in such value-laden terms as careerism or middle-class individualism. Indeed, many had not been overly concerned with promotion until they had experienced the vagaries of the system and dissatisfaction with grade had no bearing either way on the strength of the lecturers' felt need for trade unionism for teachers.

Despite the strength of feeling about both the system of grades and their salaries, it has to be said that it was not enough to generate positive dissatisfaction with teaching as a career on the part of most lecturers. Indeed only 8 per cent of the sample were prepared to say they were unhappy with their choice of career and a further 22 per cent were unsure. This was because despite dissatisfaction over extrinsic rewards, the job offered the opportunity to experience a variety of intrinsic rewards which the lecturers obviously valued and which had obviously been part of their motivation in taking up teaching in the first place:

> I always wanted to teach. I now feel that I am at last doing something useful. I enjoy my work thoroughly.
>
> Lecturer I, aged 23, Office Skills

> It is the most arduous job I have ever undertaken and yet it is the most satisfying and rewarding.
>
> Lecturer I, aged 33, Motor Vehicle Mechanics

> I feel complete satisfaction and fulfilment in my work. I particularly enjoy contact with students whose response to my efforts I find rewarding and enjoyable.
>
> Senior Lecturer, aged 33, Polytechnic

I have learnt more than I have taught! The work is
so unpredictable and the students so different and
uniformly pleasant and the work they do so lively
and stimulating, that I never tire of the job.
                              Senior Lecturer, aged 41, Design

Often, many intrinsic factors seemed to combine to produce
an intensity of job satisfaction found in few occupations
outside teaching. In fact the college lecturers made explicit
comparisons with their previous occupations:

I found little scope during my years in industry.
The amount of chemistry actually used was very
small.
                              Lecturer II, aged 44, Polytechnic

After industry and the Civil Service etc. I have had
a glimpse of other careers. I prefer teaching, so
satisfying and rewarding.
                    Senior Lecturer, aged 43, Management Studies

I know the alternatives!
                    Lecturer II, aged 39, Production Engineering

On the whole the evidence would seem to suggest that
the majority of college lecturers had a highly intrinsic
orientation to work. Intrinsic factors were by far the most
important factors both in 'pushing' lecturers out of their
previous occupations and in 'pulling' them into teaching.
Certainly there was little evidence to suggest that the
majority of lecturers, as individuals, were overly careerist
in orientation with little normative commitment to their
work, as Tipton, for example, has argued in her study of
technical college staff. At her college, she argued, the
lecturers:

neither worked for an institution with a cherished
special image; nor were held tightly together by a
shared understanding and mutual economic
interests; were relatively weak on moral involvement in teaching; were relatively strong on
commitment to extrinsic rewards.[20]

We have seen how certain structural features of the
profession, in particular the method of calculating establish-

ments and the system of graded posts, can be a source of disunity and great resentment in the colleges but to elevate these aspects of the lecturers' relationship to their work to the level of its defining characteristic would represent at best only a partial truth. For despite their dissatisfaction with extrinsic rewards, such dissatisfactions were in most cases not sufficient to influence the lecturers' overall satisfaction with teaching as a career, an inconsistency which can only be resolved with reference to the enormous scope for intrinsic rewards which teaching has to offer. It could not therefore be said of college lecturers, as it has been of manual workers, that at work their natural state is one of discontent.[21]

BUREAUCRATIC HIERARCHY

It has been argued that professionalism as articulated within the protective associations of professional employees represented an anti-trade union status-ideology rather than a job specification or orientation to work. But if we define professionalism as an occupational role based upon a high level of expertise and a commitment to the autonomous exercise of that expertise (subject only to the authority of professional peers), how far was work in the colleges organised on a professional basis and to what extent did lecturers have a professional orientation to work? There is evidence to suggest that at the very time when professionalism as an ideology was in the ascendancy in the ATTI, the organisation of work and the orientation of lecturers at college level were anything but professional. We have already seen that the rank and file lecturers in the years before the Second World War were reluctant to take advantage of the various reforms in examinations which would allow them greater control over the content of their courses. But if the lecturers lacked confidence in their own professional expertise, so too did the accreditation bodies. In 1914, the president of the ATTI made a long and passionate plea for the abolition of external examinations and for the setting up of advisory boards with strong teacher representation to be concerned with both syllabi and examinations. He explained the proliferation of external examining bodies in terms of the authorities' distrust of the teacher:

> The idea that a teacher should assist in the examination of his own pupils is one which fills

their minds with horror and distrust ... This distrust
inevitably implies that the work of the teacher
throughout the course is to be tested by means of
an examination ... The true function of the
examination is that it is one of several factors by
means of which the teacher is to satisfy himself
that the pupil has worked satisfactorily. To regard
it as a test of the teachers is a topsy-turvey idea,
and if it is utilised as such, then you are inflicting
a severe handicap upon educational progress.[22]

And the situation which existed in relation to external
examinations prior to the Second World War was graphically
summed up (some time later) in the Technical Journal:

It was a system in which teachers, often untrained
assistants, doled out to tired evening students
doses of bookish technical instruction prescribed
minutely in 'syllabuses' handed down by remote
authorities called 'examiners', after which students
regurgitated quantities of this matter in papers set
and marked by these same mandarins. Teachers for
the most part were mere operatives in the
process.[23]

The ATTI was also concerned to wrest the colleges
from the detailed control of the local authorities which
reserved the right to appoint academic staff and allowed
little discretion over such everyday administrative tasks as
the ordering of equipment. Significantly, however, there was
little discussion about the relations between the different
grades of staff within the colleges. Little was said, for
example, about the rights of the rank and file teacher to
have a say in academic policy-making, rights which would
seem to have been reserved for the governing body (where
one existed) and the principal should the governing body be
willing. Richardson, himself a college principal, hinted at
the autocratic relations which could exist between a
principal and his staff in his pre-war handbook of technical
education:

A Principal should delegate completely the
responsibility for the work of a Department to its
appointed Head. This, I fear, is not always done. If
the Principal interferes with the Head in the

control of his Department he will only create difficulties and may commute enthusiasm into indifference ... The greatness of an institution is never due to the effort of a single individual, it is the product of many minds working together. The Principal who tries to do the work of his staff as well as his own, or to take credit for work that is not his, is unlikely to be the Head of a progressive or enlightened institution.[24]

Venables is somewhat more explicit when he refers to the pre-war years as 'the days of the authoritarian principal or head laying down the law from on high, with no explanation given if anyone dared ask'.[25] The reality of the power of the principal during these years is reflected in the many calls for a restriction of their rights within the Association and even for their exclusion from membership. On the other hand, the leadership of the Association, themselves senior members of staff, were always adamant in their opposition to such moves, convinced as they were in the 'professional' nature of the Association.

The general lack of true professional status and control both on the part of the colleges as institutions and the lecturers as teachers seems to have continued into the post-war years. Venables, for example, constantly laments the lack of teacher representation in technical education in the immediate post-war years and attacks the reluctance of the local authorities to loosen the reins on the colleges through the devolution of power to properly constituted governing bodies. The need for this had been officially recognised in 1946 when Circular 98 proposed that governing bodies should be so constituted as to enjoy the freedom 'to develop its work in such directions as prove desirable and to attract first class members of staff'.[26] But an enquiry conducted in 1954 showed that of the 198 colleges surveyed, 136 had governing bodies which were, in their strictly limited powers, 'but sub-committees of sub-committees of the education committees concerned'.[27] Conscious of the constraints which might be imposed on the colleges in these circumstances, the Ministry of Education stepped in again with Circular 7/59 which recommended that colleges be given 'independence appropriate to their level of work' and by the sixties most colleges had some form of governing body.[28] The extent to which many represented a real devolution of power from the local authority is, however, questionable. According to Robinson, for example, there still existed in the sixties authorities which treated governing bodies as 'mere advisory committees with virtually no power'. Robinson also suggests that there was often little opposition from senior staff to such local authority control over the colleges and goes as far as to claim that they themselves might ultimately be the greatest obstacle to reform, finding as they did 'security in the lack of responsibility which accompanies the withholding of power'.[29]

But if autonomy in the face of the local authorities was rare, then the opportunity for more junior members of staff to participate in decision-making was even rarer. For example, a detailed study of administration in six colleges in the sixties revealed that not one could boast a staff representative other than the principal on the governing body.[30] Indeed, Burgess and Pratt claim that the rigidly hierarchical external relations which characterised the administration of the colleges during this period were mirrored inside the colleges. Relations between junior and senior staff remained autocratic and junior staff were not expected to interest themselves in matters of policy. Often, we are told, a principal might not think it necessary to inform, let alone consult, junior staff on academic and other developments.[31] Here Burgess and Pratt echo the concerns of Ethel Venables who in her study of a local technical college adds, importantly, that 'the principal who accepts unquestionably the restriction of his own powers tends not to involve his own staff in decisions affecting their work'.[32]

It was with such considerations as these in mind that the 1968 Education Act (No. 2) was passed requiring the representation of staff other than the principal on governing bodies and the development of academic boards to facilitate the participation of all academic staff in academic decision-making. Designation of Polytechnic status was made conditional upon instruments and articles of government incorporating such principles and with Circular 7/70 they were made to apply to all colleges in the public sector regardless of level of work taught. By the seventies, then, the formal opportunities for the lecturers to exercise professional autonomy and control were greatly improved although it soon became apparent that the proposals incorporated in Circular 7/70 could not guarantee the democratisation of the colleges. An ATTI survey in 1972, for example, found that many colleges, especially in London, had Academic Boards which remained advisory to the principal and whilst Circular 7/70 recommended that a significant proportion of the seats go to staff elected by the college as a whole, senior members of staff and staff co-opted by senior members of staff tended to predominate. And here is the nub of the problem. Whilst relations between junior and senior staff on the college floor might now be less autocratic, for as long as the system of graded posts was untouched, they remained, nevertheless, hierarchical and this had important implications for college democracy.

Senior members of staff are invested with a control over those more junior not unlike that of management in any enterprise. Whilst it is very difficult to actually sack a college lecturer, senior colleagues have considerable influence over promotion prospects, these being decided by the principal in consultation with heads of department. Neither do the frontiers of control stop at the heads of department. With the proliferation of teaching grades since the fifties, other senior staff are invested with administrative functions which involve an element of control. Course directors, for example, might well be expected to make recommendations for promotion. They might also be in the position of putting additional administrative responsibilities in the way of individual lecturers, important given that administrative duties are a major avenue of promotion in most colleges. Given this dependence of junior staff on the 'goodwill' of more senior colleagues, they might well be reluctant to express opinions on academic policy at odds with them. The contradictions of participation within a hierarchical structure were well summed up at the time by the magazine 'Further Left' which remained unimpressed by Circular 7/70:

> Staff on college committees are likely to suffer from their own inexperience and timidity. They are likely to be kept in ignorance of decisively important information. Too often, being elected as a 'staff representative' is seen as a means of advancing a career and not a few may be expected to be 'bought off'. The career structure helps to ensure that little which is really unpopular with the authorities is said even by the most conscientious junior teacher - since only the bravest will jeopardise their chances of promotion.[33]

Countless articles and letters in The NATFHE Journal since have pointed to the lack of reality of democracy in a 'system which allows those in authority to operate power through patronage'.[34] Such a situation would indicate the continued existence in the colleges of what Blau and Scott have called a 'bureaucratic' (as opposed to professional) control structure; that is, a control structure based on a hierarchy of authority derived from organisational role rather than the professional peer group.[35]

Given such a bureaucratic control structure, the strong implication is that lecturers might feel that their interests in college would be best served by building up 'special relationships' with senior colleagues rather than by allowing the union to regulate work relationships in a collective manner. Furthermore, such an attitude is likely to be sustained by competition for resources both between departments within the same college and within colleges in the same catchment area. The go-ahead for new courses, accommodation and generous time allowances for them can all depend on having a strong head of department or course director who can fight for them in the appropriate committee. So too with promotions. The existence of sectional interests both within and between colleges combined with the proliferation of teaching grades based on bureaucratic principles of control can result in an situation where heads of department and other senior members of staff can in a very real sense protect the interests of those more junior. Even a principal can act and be seen to act in their interests by 'cooking the books' or by aggressive public relations work in favour of the institution. Add to this the lack of any clear conflict of goal within the colleges (all being, in theory at least, 'for the good of' the subject, the department, the college, or the students) then despite a bureaucratic control structure and the fact that senior colleagues are charged with running the colleges within the limits laid down by the employers, there is no clear differentiation between management and staff on the college floor. It is likely under these circumstances that lecturers might tend to view internal college relations in 'unitary' rather than 'oppositional' terms and see only a limited role for the union branch in terms of job regulation.

MANAGEMENT'S RIGHT TO MANAGE
Indeed, it was apparent from the field work that this could be a real problem for the union at branch level. The

following themes were constantly repeated by those critical of the limited union activity in their college:

> I feel that union officials should not be concerned about maintaining good relations. A more militant and perhaps more obnoxious approach would bring more success.
>
> Lecturer I, aged 31, Liberal Studies

> Generally would be more successful by taking a stronger line with principal, vice-principal, heads of department, on a wide range of matters concerning shop floor staff.
>
> Senior Lecturer, aged 61, Foundry Technology

> By being less subservient to the principal/LEA.
>
> Senior Lecturer, aged 42, Economics

Some explained the passivity of their branch in terms of the senior staff in official positions, but others thought that branch officers could do little without the support of the membership as a whole:

> The basic problem is the relatively poor attendance at meetings and the general lack of interest in the ATTI. It should take more of a day to day interest in conditions, relations with Admin., promotions etc., but it is insufficiently supported to do this well.
>
> Lecturer II, aged 31, Polytechnic

> Increase the solidarity amongst the staff so they give more support to one another. Staff are afraid to oppose higher levels for fear of promotion prospects.
>
> Lecturer I, aged 23, Sociology

Two branches in Manchester illustrated the dynamics of local branch activity during the period when the ATTI nationally was consolidating its character as a trade union. The first, a local college, was led by committed union activists who found it very difficult to convince the members of their belief that every area of negotiation between junior and senior colleagues was a legitimate area for union intervention. The branch chairman, for example, was concerned that:

> The branch should put emphasis on being a trade
> union. It must be an active, relevant body and aim
> to be strong and be seen to be strong. Members
> should be on every single body concerned with
> teachers' rights ... the academic board, governing
> body. Staff members should be ATTI sponsored
> under mandate ... As members of a department we
> have no control over resources and finance. The
> branch should have more control. But the difficulty
> is to know how to achieve it. The apathy has to be
> seen to be believed. There's lots of griping,
> especially about conditons of service, but they
> won't do anything. A resolution was passed through
> the branch not to substitute because it's unpaid
> overtime. It was totally ignored. They've been
> promised payment, but they won't get it. Certain
> members were promoted but they didn't get any
> back pay. We threatened a massive strike and got
> our way, but it was all bluff.

The issue of ATTI representation on the Academic Board
was very much a live one at this college at the time. The
activists felt that they were losing the issue because departmental representatives, mostly senior lecturers, were too
concerned to represent the sectional interests of their
department and in this they had the backing of the departmental staff. The activists, on the other hand, believed that
the union was the only body which could, and should,
represent the teachers as a whole.

The staff were obviously divided as to whether this was
the right approach to take. Indeed a one-time activist,
though careful to point out he was a socialist, had dropped
out of college politics altogether because:

> The branch meeting has ceased to be
> representative ... I don't go any more because I
> don't find meetings congenial. I'm a socialist
> alright but I regret the sledge-hammer tactics to
> crack small eggs. For example, there was a huge
> confrontation over a member's room being taken
> away from him. All it needed was a quiet word
> with the Principal, but the union jumped on it. The
> academic board is another case in point. We're too

small a college for such a union intervention. It might be OK in a large college where Heads and the Principal to some extent substitute for the employer. But here we work together. They're not like employers here. Employers generally only succumb to force. But here the Principal and Local Authorities are on our side. But their hands are tied by the government which hides behind their backs.

On the other hand, another one-time activist at the same college had dropped out of college politics for exactly the opposite reasons. He used to be the branch secretary but had given it up because his militancy had caused so much bad feeling he found it personally too difficult a role to sustain. A live issue for him at that moment was that of career's guidance which he felt was fundamental to the well-being of the students but he could get no recognition of this in terms of time allowance or accommodation:

> The branch is helpless in the face of an intran-sigent administration on local issues. They think it's none of your business. We take the decisions, you can only advise ... There's no esprit de corps here, no concept of fighting the boss. You hardly get a quorum at branch meetings. On conditions of service you're up against Admin. all the time - they want maximum use of facilities. The more students you can pack in the better. It's not in the interests of good teaching. Everything's subjective here. There's a lot of careerists looking out for themselves. To them the Principal can do no wrong. They have no cohesive philosophy of education. Merely, how does it affect me? That's why they don't want ATTI reps. on the academic board. Staff are outnumbered by admin. and would-be admin. The boss gives all the leads and they take the signals from him.

He then apologised for his outburst: 'I haven't always been militant, it's just years of coming up against a brick wall.'
Compare this situation with one in an area college in Manchester where the local union leadership had been very much part of the college establishment. Nearly all the lecturers spoken to complained of the ATTI being a bosses'

union. This was probably due to the fact that almost the whole of the printing department had previously resigned over a dispute with their head of department. The union had refused to take the matter up, they believed, because their head of department was a 'big-wig' in the ATTI. As one lecturer involved in the dispute put it:

> This is no union. It's a professional association ... You've got the bosses in the same union, heads of department and principals. Eighty per cent of disputes are with the heads of department. Both sides can't take it to the union. The union should take your side regardless. You need machinery like that of a shop steward ... You can't tell the union anything in confidence. You can't trust them because they're on the side of the bosses.

In this light it was interesting to meet the former branch secretary who had presided over the branch during the period when this negative attitude had built up. He was a Conservative Party councillor and a principal lecturer who was rather bored with teaching by this time but who had not left because, as a principal lecturer, it gave him enough time to play the stock market and ply his trade in life insurance. He would not go out on strike over pay because he found the idea of striking just over pay distasteful and anyway, he believed a person should be paid at his replacement value and 'it was his hard luck' if he was not worth much. Before entering teaching he had refused to join a union because they protected the bad worker, but the ATTI had struck him as being a responsible body and this was why he had been a branch secretary and departmental representative for many years. After the interview, he asked whether I had the principal's permission to talk to the college staff. He thought I should have as I was, after all, speaking to lecturers who were his staff in what was, effectively, college time. The new branch secretary, however, was indignant at the very suggestion. I was the guest of the union and it was none of the principal's business. This as much as anything else sums up the difference in outlook between the former branch secretary, who might well have been one of those referred to as 'the corrupt brigade who used their union position to get on' and the present incumbent who was considered 'a good bloke' and the reason why many had rejoined the union. Rather than accepting the rights and prerogatives of management as the former branch secretary obviously did, the new branch secretary was more concerned to build up the union's independence from management as a force to be reckoned with.

What was most interesting from this point of view was the evidence to suggest that some lecturers might reject ATTI intervention in areas considered by others to be legitimate areas of union concern not simply because of the possibilities of individual negotiation but because they believed them to be the prerogative of management to determine. In other words, they accepted 'management's right to manage'. Take the group of women lecturers at the local college in Manchester who were adamantly against the branch officers' attempts at job regulation on the college floor and who expressed their disapproval with such remarks as:

> The Head of Department's the gaffer. He's in charge. Even if I disagreed, I'd accept his word.

> It's part of the job to have to substitute, to do registers and so on ... You know what to expect when you come here. If you don't like it, you can always leave.

> You expect to be consulted, but he's [the Head of Department] the boss. That's what he's paid for. To take decisions.

Such attitudes as these expressed what Corwin has called a passive 'employee mentality' rather than a professional orientation to work.[36] It was an attitude which was increasingly breaking down during the period in question giving rise to crises of authority in many institutions. Such crises of authority were epitomised in the 'Guildford Dispute', a dispute which was recognised as a watershed in the fight for college democracy in that it gave rise to the provisions of Circular 7/70.

During August 1968, seven full-time and 33 part-time lecturers were sacked from the Guildford School of Art following a student sit-in. The sit-in was essentially a protest about the nature of art education and the courses offered by the college, a malaise shared by many members of the staff. However, neither the students nor the staff had any legitimate means of voicing their grievances.

According to one of the lecturers sacked:

> Control at Guildford was wholly in the hands of the
> Governors, the Principal and a very small number
> of favoured senior staff. There were no staff
> meetings (not for ten years) and no proper
> meetings of Heads of Department, and no
> academic board. Staff were not even informed,
> never mind consulted, about the merger with the
> nearby Farnham School of Art. When the whole of
> the staff met together on 12th June 1968 they
> unanimously agreed upon plans for a staff-student
> consultative structure designed to restore the
> School to normality. The Governors ignored the
> proposals.[37]

The Governors ignored the proposals because they had
already agreed an alternative course of action. At a
confidential meeting two days before they had resolved:

> That as the Governors feel that it is necessary for
> the speedy and effective resolution of present
> difficulties that the Principal should have the
> unqualified support of all members of the full-time
> staff at the College, those members who cannot
> give him such support shall be liable to suspension
> by the Principal acting for and with the authority
> of the Governors, which authority is hereby
> given.[38]

The Governors then closed the school and demanded that the
staff, many of whom had been participating in the debates
during the sit-in, should not enter. Those that did were
sacked for 'professional misconduct'. The sacked teachers,
on the other hand, claimed that their professional
responsibility was to their students and to art education, not
to the principal and governing body:

> In effect, the Authority resolved deep differences
> about the teaching of art and the nature of college
> government at Guildford by sacking the teachers
> whose opinions it did not agree with ... There was
> never any question of the staff meekly vacating
> the premises and deserting their students, we
> stayed because the educational issues involved

were of greater significance than our employers'
petty regulations. What we regarded as the
assertion of the rights and responsibilities of
teachers, they considered an act of 'professional
misconduct'.[39]

The ATTI nationally gave full support to the sacked teachers
operating, amongst other things, a blacklist against their
employer. There was a strong feeling at the time, however,
that many rank and file lecturers were not so sympathetic
and that a significant minority at least did indeed believe
that the college authorities had a right to expect loyalty
from their staff. In other words, they believed in management's right to manage rather than in the professional right
to exercise autonomous discretion and control.

Students of American teacher unionism have argued
that such an 'employee mentality' on the part of American
teachers is conducive to a passive, compliant attitude
towards the administration, an attitude which is unlikely to
favour either trade unionism in the form of job regulation on
the college floor or the desire for professional autonomy and
control.[40] The survey data would seem to indicate that the
same has been true for college lecturers here. A measure of
professional orientation to work was achieved by asking the
lecturers how much decision-making power teachers should
have in relation to both senior colleagues and outside bodies.
Those lecturers who thought that teachers should either
have more say or an equal voice were thought to have a
professional orientation to work. This was then cross-
tabulated with lecturers' attitudes to the rights of college
authorities to demand loyalty from their staff (the index of
an 'employee mentality'). The lecturers who were concerned
to exercise professional control over their work were
extremely unlikely to accept that college authorities had a
right to demand loyalty from their staff. On the other hand,
they were significantly more likely to believe that the
college administration would not look after their interests
so well if there were no ATTI branch in college and much
more willing to see their branch intervene in internal
college affairs. Furthermore, those with a professional
orientation to work were more likely to want ATTI
representation on the academic board and happier to see the
ATTI branch use militant tactics to achieve lecturers' goals.
It would seem then that professionalism as orientation to
work and trade unionism on the college floor are not in

contradiction, as the old-guard in the Association would have had us believe. On the contrary, the more professional in orientation the lecturers were, the more likely they were to see the need for strong union representation, a finding which would lend further support to the argument that objections to it on traditional professional grounds have been more ideological than real in content.

NOTES

1. G.S. Bain et al., Social Stratification and Trade Unionism (Heinemann, 1973), p.13.

2. The interview and survey data in this chapter are drawn from fieldwork carried out during the period 1973 to 1976.

3. There was general agreement about the influence of youth within the Association. Whilst the overall age distribution within the profession changed very little during the years of expansion, the mere rate of that expansion brought a huge increase in the absolute numbers of young recruits. From this group came the first organised left-wing within the Association centred around the magazine Further Left, a magazine which was committed to 'militant action against Tory policies and support for trade union principles in teacher associations'.

4. Bain et al., Social Stratification, p.95.

5. David Lockwood, The Blackcoated Worker (Allen & Unwin, 1958), p.195.

6. C. Wright Mills, White Collar (Oxford University Press, 1951).

7. B.C. Roberts et al., Reluctant Militants (Heinemann, 1972).

8. Bob Carter, 'Trade Unionism and the New Middle Class - The Case of ASTMS' in Peter Armstrong et al., White Collar Workers, Trade Unions and Class (Croom Helm, 1986), pp.132-59.

9. R.H. Blackburn & M. Mann, 'Ideology in the Non-skilled Working Class' in M. Bulmer (ed), Working Class Images of Society (Routledge and Kegan Paul, 1975), p.155.

10. Ibid.

11. For useful summaries of the 'new middle-class' position see Peter Armstrong et al., White Collar Workers, and R. Hyman & R. Price, The New Working Class (Macmillan, 1983). For a critique of its application where professional workers in general and teachers in particular

are concerned see J. Ogza & M. Lawn, Teachers, Professionalism and Class (Falmer Press, 1981), pp.39-63.

12. Ogza & Lawn, Teachers, Professionalism and Class, p.50.

13. Chris Smith, 'Engineers, Trade Unionism and Tass' in Peter Armstrong et al., pp.160-97.

14. Robert Price, 'White-Collar Unions: Growth, Character and Attitudes in the 1970s' in Hyman & Price, The New Working Class, 1983, pp.147-83.

15. Richard Hyman and Ian Brough, Social Values and Industrial Relations (Blackwell, 1975).

16. Ibid. p.37.

17. A study undertaken by the National Foundation for Educational Research in 1979 confirms this view. Focussing on further education as a career and drawing on data from questionnaires, interviews and group discussion involving over 3,500 teachers, it concluded that the opportunities and criteria for promotion in FE were a source of some considerable dissatisfaction and that there was an urgent need for reform. See Judy Bradley & Jane Silverleaf, Making the Grade: Careers in Further Education (NFER, 1979).

18. Roberts, Reluctant Militants, p.117.

19. H.A. Blalock, 'Status Consciousness: A Dimensional Analysis', Social Forces, no. 37 (1959), pp.243-8.

20. Beryl Tipton, 'Some Organisational Characteristics of a Technical College', Research in Education, no. 7 (May 1972).

21. Describing the lot of the industrial worker, Harbison, for example, wrote:

> The industrial worker, for the most part, works harder than he likes at tasks which are frequently arduous, usually monotonous and sometimes dangerous. On the job he is nearly always subject to the direction of higher authority. His income is seldom sufficient to cover what he thinks his needs demand. The natural state of the industrial worker is one of discontent.

F.H. Harbison, 'Collective Bargaining and American Capitalism' in A. Kornhauser et al., Industrial Conflict (McGraw Hill, 1954).

22. Technical Journal, July 1914.

23. Ibid. June 1964.

24. W.A. Richardson, The Technical College, its

Organisation and Administration (Oxford University Press, 1939) p.131.

25. Peter Venables, Technical Education, Its Aims, Organisation and Future Development (Bell, 1956), p.503.

26. Ibid. p.484.

27. Ibid. pp.485-6.

28. For a useful account of changing official attitudes to college government during this period see Michael Locke, 'Government' in J. Pratt & T. Burgess, Polytechnics: A Report (Pitman, 1974), pp.149-71.

29. Eric Robinson, The New Polytechnics (Penguin, 1968), p.121.

30. D. Charlton, W. Gent and B. Scammells, The Administration of Technical Colleges (Manchester University Press, 1971).

31. T. Burgess and J. Pratt, Policy and Practice (Allen Lane, 1970), p.134.

32. Ethel Venables, The Young Worker at College (Faber, 1967), p.118.

33. 'College Democratisation, What Next?' Further Left, November 1971.

34. See, for example, articles on college democracy in The NATFHE Journal, October 1981, November 1982 and March/April 1983.

35. Peter Blau and Richard W. Scott, Formal Organisations: A Comparative Approach (Routledge and Kegan Paul, 1963). The distinction between bureaucratic and professional principles of organisation led many sociologists to focus on the ways in which professionals adjust to organisational demands. See, for example, the readings in A. Etzioni (ed), The Semi-Professions and their Organisation: Teachers, Nurses and Social Workers (Collier-Macmillan, 1969).

36. R.G. Corwin, Militant Professionalism (Appleton-Century-Crofts, 1970), pp.7-8.

37. I am grateful to Mike Stedman, one of the lecturers sacked during the affair, for furnishing me with papers he had written for internal ATTI consumption.

38. Minutes of the Governors' Meeting, 10 June 1968. Cited in Mike Stedman, 'The Guildford Affair', unpublished paper, 1968.

39. Ibid.

40. See, for example, Corwin, Militant Professionalism and M. Liebermann, Education as a Profession (Prentice-Hall, 1956).

6
A Future Secured?

PROFESSIONAL TRADE UNIONISM

It has been apparent from the history of both the technical teachers and technical teaching that the fate of both was inextricably linked. In this sense the early technical teachers were right in the importance they lent to the education function of their Association. Where they were wrong was in believing that both the fate of their service and their material well-being could be ensured by stressing the unity of interest which they felt existed between themselves and their employers. At one level this unity might indeed exist, particularly where a local authority or the government of the day has made a political commitment to that sector of education. It remains true, however, that in a society governed by the economic laws of capital and moreover where those laws are operating with increasing inefficiency, both the teachers and the service they represent will come under attack. In this respect, 'harmonistic collectivism' as an occupational strategy was difficult to sustain in the face of the reality of the lecturers' employee status. Whatever their relative market or status positions, they were not independent professionals selling their services directly to a client and whether they wanted to protect either the quality of their service or their material well-being they were, in the final analysis, at the mercy of their employer just like any other employee. Whilst they struggled for years for a Teachers' Council to determine entry into the profession, the government always refused because, as Beatrice Webb argued, that would be tantamount to allowing employees to control salaries and terms of service according to their own discretion. It was then, the college lecturers' impotence as employees rather than their status as professionals which determined their association's development into a much more union-like body.

Nevertheless, it was in the nature of their work as professionals that their trade union should concern itself with the quality of the service which they offered. By the

166

time that the ATTI merged with the Association of Teachers in Colleges and Departments of Education (ATCDE) in January 1976 to become the National Association of Teachers in Further and Higher Education (NATFHE), it had already become a whole-hearted 'professional trade union', its leadership both educationalists and trade unionists in the fullest sense. Indeed the education secretary of the new Association was optimistic about the role it could now play in the development of progressive education policies. Admitting ruefully that once the Association's education policies had indeed developed with at least one eye to improving the conditions of service of the membership, he believed that now that the future of further education was secure, the Association could concentrate more purely on issues of social justice.

Such optimism was ill-founded. Even as NATFHE was coming into being, it was clear that the era of unbridled expansion was over and that a period of resource constraint would have a significant impact on provision. The first major casualty was teacher training. This had become NATFHE's responsibility with its inclusion in the Further Education Regulations of 1975 consequent upon a commitment to integrate teacher education into the mainstream of public sector higher education in The James Report (1971) and the White Paper, Higher Education: a Framework for Expansion (1972). NATFHE approved the reorganisation of teacher education but quarrelled with the extent of reductions in initial teacher training as official targets fell from between 60,000-70,000 in 1972 to between 34,000-36,000 in 1977. Projections for in-service training fell from 15,000 full-time equivalent places to 10,000-12,000. Such projections were based on the known fall in the birth-rate and growing evidence of unemployment amongst teachers, particularly those newly qualified. Such was the situation that teacher education suffered progressive cutbacks culminating in the massive programme of course closures and college mergers announced by the Secretary of State in January 1977. NATFHE estimated that some 3,500 jobs would be lost in teacher education over the following four years.[1]

In the face of the known facts, it was difficult to oppose the cuts outright even though many believed that the rate of teacher unemployment was the result of political rather than demographic factors. The period was one of successive public expenditure cuts. In December 1973, the

A Future Secured?

'Barber Cuts' took £182 million from the education budget and set an average growth rate of 4.8 per cent. Healey's 1974 interim budget restricted growth in education spending to 4 per cent in real terms for 1975/6 and set an average growth rate in public expenditure of 2.75 per cent for 1974/5 to 1978/9. In April 1975 the regular budget took £86 million off education spending for 1976/7 and in the following February a total cutback of £620 million was mooted for the period up to 1978/9.

Cuts in central funding were compounded by increasing restrictions on local authority expenditure. Government Circular 10/75 announced that local authorities had overspent and that there would, therefore, be a policy of nil growth in 1976/7. November 1975 saw the first cuts in the Rate Support Grant with central government's contribution to education reduced from 66.5 per cent to 65.5 per cent. The following year saw it cut again to 61 per cent. Furthermore, strict cash limits were imposed on any increases to allow for inflation. In such a climate as this, it was highly unlikely that any excess in teacher supply would be used to improve staffing levels in the 45 per cent of primary and 15 per cent of secondary school classes estimated by NATFHE to have over 30 pupils, or that any excess capacity in the colleges themselves would be used to improve in-service training, as NATFHE had argued it should.

For all these reasons, the major thrust of NATFHE's response to the crisis in teacher education was to negotiate favourable early retirement for lecturers over 50 and redeployment for the rest. It was especially concerned that the loss of teacher training places should not result in a loss of provision in higher education as a whole and that alternative places be provided through diversified courses. To a certain extent this did in fact happen as the overall number of students in higher education was expected to rise over the next few years (the 18 year-old age group was expected to peak in 1982-3 and fall thereafter by a rapid 40 per cent) despite the cutback in teacher training. Indeed, in April the following year, the Secretary of State for Higher Education, Gordon Oakes, pointed out that whilst overall public sector numbers in higher education were not expected to increase very much to 1981-2, non-teacher training figures were planned to increase by about 39 per cent and it was out of the closure of some 30 colleges of education and the amalgamation of others that the Colleges and Institutes of Higher Education were created in the late seventies to meet this demand. Nevertheless, in the immediate, the dramatic reduction in teacher education places resulted in a net loss for higher education.

At the same time, official projections for higher education were becoming increasingly gloomy. In 1972, the Conservative government's White Paper, A Framework for Expansion, had projected 750,000 student places for 1981. The Labour government revised this figure downwards to 640,000 in 1974 and 600,000 in 1976 on the grounds of reduced demand. These figures were reduced further still in their discussion document, Higher Education into the 1990s, published in 1978. This document was heavily criticised for both its over-emphasis on demographic factors as the determinant of provision in higher education and its static concept of student demand, although it did put forward an expansionist option for consideration (Model E). Indeed, Gordon Oakes, spoke to NATFHE conference that year on the desirability of just such a model to increase participation in higher education amongst those groups traditionally under-represented and announced the government's agreement in principle to educational allowances for students beyond 16 as just one way in which demand might be stimulated. Nevertheless, by the time of its follow-up report, Future Trends in Higher Education, a year later, many believed that Model E had been abandoned in favour of a concept of demand defined 'solely in terms of the traditional demand by the traditional age-group on traditional full-time courses'.[2] In consequence, student numbers in higher education were put at between 540,000–580,000 for the mid-1980s and a steady decline thereafter was predicted.

NATFHE argued against these pessimistic projections on the grounds that the age participation rate (the number of home entrants under 21 as a percentage of that age-group) in higher education was already lower than that of Britain's major competitors and had actually dropped from 14 per cent in 1973/4 to 13.1 per cent in 1977/8. The need was to stimulate demand rather than plan for its decline and there were client groups other than the traditional 18-21 age-group which would continue to grow at least until the end of the century. In this respect, great emphasis was placed on the continuing education of the adult population and the effect which technological change and unemployment might have on the need for retraining. Above all, access to higher education should be more open to increase the opportunities to those disadvantaged by class, age, sex and ethnic origin. In fact, demand did indeed begin to grow in the 1980s, at least in part from just such groups. As can be seen from Table 6.1, this resulted in a significant increase in student numbers in public sector higher education once the cutbacks in teacher training places had worked their way through. Furthermore, and despite ominous hints to the contrary in Future Trends, these increases were greater than those in the university sector. In 1980, for example, 51 per cent of first-year home students entered the universities. By 1983, this proportion had dropped to 44 per cent.

Tale 6.1: Home students on full-time, sandwich and part-time courses in higher education in Great Britain, 1975-1983 (nos. in thousands)

	1975	1980	1981	1982	1983
Public Sector:					
Full-time	226.1	202.6	223.3	242.7	259.9
Part-time	134.1	188.5	191.7	194.6	200.8
All home students	360.3	391.2	415.0	437.3	460.7
Universities:					
Full-time	230.1	265.4	268.4	264.5	259.5
Part-time	25.0	31.9	33.2	33.5	34.6
Open University	56.0	67.8	71.0	74.5	76.1
All home students	311.1	365.1	372.6	372.5	370.3

Source: DES Statistical Bulletin, 9/85

First indications for 1984 were that the total student numbers in higher education would be 1 per cent more than in 1983 with a further small decrease in university numbers offset by the increase in the public sector. The relatively greater growth in student numbers in the public sector was in part due to its greater flexibility in dealing with less orthodox students on a wide range of courses (in this respect it is interesting to note the reversal of the previous downward trend in part-time student numbers) and in part due to the severe cutbacks which the universities themselves suffered in the early eighties. Nevertheless, these increased numbers were achieved in conditions somewhat less than favourable to NATFHE and its members.

In 1979, the first Thatcher government came to power committed to monetarist economic policies and a weakening of the strength of the trade union movement. During the term of office of the previous Labour government there had been cuts in public expenditure enough and NATFHE had joined with other trade unions, particularly those in the public sector, to demonstrate against them. At the same time, it had been concerned to challenge the prevailing economic orthodoxy that the cuts were necessary to bring Britain out of its ever deepening recession. Even so, after the Tories took £55 million off the education budget almost immediately on coming to office, many, not least among the Association's membership, were prepared to believe that the cuts were still a temporary phenomenon designed, as the government said, to revitalise British industry. However, when in July the cabinet agreed to cut planned expenditure for 1980/1 by £4,000 million with possibly greater cuts after that and in early September possible cuts of 10,15 and 20 per cent in the major spending departments were examined, it became apparent that 'Thatcherism' represented something more than just a few more years of belt-tightening. And when Dr. Rhodes Boyson, Under-secretary of State for Higher Education, announced on the occasion of a 6 per cent cut in university expenditure that the Robbins principle was nothing more than a 'mad dream',[3] it was clear that the Association had a major battle on its hands.

In the event, however, that battle was not fought over student numbers but over resources. Early in 1980, legislation was put through Parliament which gave the government the statutory right to control what was spent on Advanced Further Education, or AFE as higher education in the public sector came increasingly to be known. Hitherto, this control had lain in the hands of the local authorities through the operation of what was known as the Advanced Further Education Pool. Under this system, expenditure on AFE was the aggregate of all the local authorities' claims. Each authority with advanced-level work contributed money to the pool according to a formula based on their school population and non-domestic rate base. They then drew out the amount it had cost them to provide such work. Central government had long been suspicious of this system believing that it encouraged local authorities to spend more

171

on higher education in the knowledge that the cost would be borne by all. With the 1980 Education Act, however, the government fixed a pre-determined amount, the 'AFE Quantum', which it would allocate each year to finance AFE. This came to be known as the 'capping' of the pool. Needless to say, given the government's commitment to spending cuts the AFE Quantum implied a progressive reduction in real terms in central government funding. If such cuts were achieved, there was, according to those within the Association with responsibility for higher education, the possibility of:

> major convulsions in higher education over the next few years, whole colleges, departments and faculties within colleges, and many courses, would have to shut down. Services to all students and the working conditions of all staff who teach and support them would be seriously weakened. Redundancies would be inevitable.[4]

With the experience of the teacher training colleges fresh in peoples' minds, such a prospect did not seem at all unlikely.

Such was the bluntness of the instrument, however, that the capping of the pool had an immediately traumatic effect on some colleges but not on others. One polytechnic's budget, for example, was cut by 1.3 million and another faced a possible job-loss of up to 240 teaching posts and a major restructuring which might include the loss of two faculties and the closure of four departments. Colleges which had expanded since 1978/9 or whose authorities had underestimated in their claim for that year were particularly badly hit. By the time of the annual conference in May 1980, the General Secretary reported that some 300 redundancy notices had already been served and that concrete proposals for redundancy existed in such authorities as Trafford, Lancashire, Surrey, Bradford, Wirral, at the North East London Polytechnic and the Polytechnic of Wales. More insidious still was the problem of what he called 'disguised redundancies', countless other lecturers who would be leaving through the misuse of Premature Retirement Compensation - 'in breach of the national agreement, without union negotiation, without union consultation, without replacement'.[5] By the end of the year, the Association had had notification of some 600 actual or potential redundancies of full-time members of staff. In addition, part-time staff had lost their contracts and vacancies had not been filled. In the words of the General Secretary, the cuts had already led to 'the slow strangling of Further and Higher Education, authority by authority and college by college'.[6] Pillage was the word used by the Association to describe the next possible cut of 10 per cent leaked to the press in October 1981, which led to predictions that a further 3,000 posts in AFE could be lost. And, once again, the suffering was not to be evenly spread, with 'high-cost' institutions suffering more than 'medium-cost' and 'low-cost' institutions 'escaping' with possible cuts of only 2 to 3 per cent. In addition, the possibility of local authority subsidy looked as if it would be lost as central government imposed stricter and stricter controls on local authority spending.

The chaos caused by the initial capping of the AFE pool led to renewed demands on the part of NATFHE for the setting up of a national planning body to oversee the whole of the public sector. A proposal for a national planning body for public sector higher education had originally been proposed towards the end of the previous Labour administration in the Oakes Report. The body proposed by Oakes represented a compromise between central and local government control and had received widespread support, not least from NATFHE, who had been promised representation. In March 1981, the press reported that new proposals were being considered at the Department of Education and Science which would take all colleges with not less than 70 per cent advanced-level work and all those concerned with initial teacher training out of the hands of the local authorities and place them under the control of a new national committee with responsibility for direct funding. The members of this committee were to be appointed by the Secretary of State in their own right, not as representatives of particular educational interests. The Under-secretary of State for Higher Education, Dr. Rhodes Boyson, made it clear that significant weight would be attached to industry and business and that the role of this new body would be to distribute the funds made available by the Exchequer in accordance with government priorities. Given the government's record to that date, the college lecturers had every reason to fear what the government's priorities might be. The memorandum itself talked of resource constraints and sharply declining numbers which would oblige higher education to contract. The Under-secretary of State had already stated that the polytechnics were originally intended to teach science and technology and that, in his opinion, they should stick to it.[7] Indeed, the government as a whole made no secret of their hostility towards the social sciences, arts and humanities. The whole tenor of their attitude towards education was that it was insufficiently geared to the country's industrial and economic needs and that much of what was being taught in higher education was icing on a cake the country could no longer afford.

NATFHE's hostility to the plan was, under the circumstances, hardly surprising:

> The Paper indicates very clearly that the Government's intention is to shrink public sector HE so that it is just meeting the perceived needs of industry as determined by a body which will have industrialists as its major voice. The Government also indicates that in order to do this, it must clearly eliminate the local authorities from any say in public sector higher education.
>
> Clearly, the capping of the AFE pool did not achieve the aims of the Government because some local authorities were sufficiently recalcitrant to actually believe in the value of their institutions, and to make up from the rates the resources they lost in order to protect their institutions' existence ... So they [the government] have now determined to ensure that, by direct institutional funding, they will be able to hack up the public sector and reduce it to what they feel to be an appropriate size and role.[8]

Whilst the Committee of Directors of Polytechnics and the Association of Polytechnic Teachers supported the plan, both the Labour Party and the local authorities were against the degree of centralisation such a body would entail and the strength of their opposition delayed any further moves until a year later when Sir Keith Joseph was appointed Secretary of State for Education and William Waldegrave his Under-secretary for Higher Education. A compromise was then reached between the requirements of national government and the interests of the local authorities and the institutions in the form of the 'National Advisory Body' (NAB). Its establishment as an interim body was announced in December 1981 and its first meetings were held early in 1982. It comprised a Committee for Local Authority Higher Education chaired by the Under-secretary of State and charged with advising the Secretary of State on the distribution of the AFE pool, and a Board which received instructions from and gave operational advice to the Committee. NATFHE took up two seats on the Board along with other institutional representatives, the CBI and the TUC. In 1985, NAB dropped its interim status and took up new responsibilities for the voluntary sector thus further incorporating teacher education into the mainstream of public sector higher education.

NAB's first major planning exercise had considerable impact on the colleges both in terms of the level and nature of provision. As many within the Association had feared, NAB was indeed successful in steering the colleges in directions determined by central government within constraints imposed by continued cuts in public expenditure. Its first major task was to process the 10 per cent cut in real terms on 1980/1 levels to be achieved by 1984/5 and, as part of the NAB's consultation exercise, institutions were invited to submit development plans which prioritised areas of work for protection from cuts. The initial basis for pool allocation rested on an institution's target student enrolments, in turn derived from an aggregate enrolment figure determined by NAB with reference to considerations on access and funding per student (the unit of resource). The final distribution was made to reflect, as far as possible, a move towards the Secretary of State's preferred subject areas of science and technology and away from the non-preferred areas such as the arts, humanities and certain social sciences. Another condition of the NAB model was that a staff-student ratio of 12:1 be achieved. The overall effect was that by the mid-eighties the trend towards the social sciences and humanities in the public sector had been reversed, the number of full-time teaching staff employed in the polytechnics had dropped from 17,845 in 1980/1 to 16,435 and the unit of resource had declined by some 24 per cent during the same period. In effect, the public sector had taken in those students who could not find places consequent upon cuts in university expenditure, but with no extra resources. The result was an additional burden on the staff, a threat to the quality of the courses and a differential of some £400 in the cost of educating a university as opposed to a polytechnic student.[9]

A Future Secured?

Neither did there seem to be much hope of a change in political climate. In 1983, the Thatcher government was elected for a second term of office. Their Green Paper, Higher Education into the 1990s (May 1985), ignored advice from the NAB that there should be a common unit of resource across the binary divide. It also rejected the recommendations on access of both the NAB and the UGC which had, in a joint statement, significantly widened the Robbins principle to make available courses in higher education 'to all those who can benefit from them and who wish to do so' thus recognising that traditional academic qualifications might not be the only or even the best predictor of potential achievement. But this principle was acceptable to the government only on the condition that the benefit was 'sufficient to justify the cost'. Furthermore, those in higher education had every reason to suspect the criteria which might be used to assess that benefit as reference was made throughout the report to the need for higher education to be tied more directly to the needs of the economy by producing more engineers and scientists on the one hand, and by developing closer links with employers on the other. It also stated that higher education should look increasingly to private rather than public finance and indicated a need for mroe specialist concentration in certain select institutions with the threat of likely closure in some others. Indeed, it proposed to take most of what remained of humanities teaching out of the colleges and into the universities thus reducing the polytechnics, bemoaned NATFHE, to their previous status of advanced technical colleges.[10]

It is irony indeed that policies which on the surface at least wished to redefine education along lines which the technical teachers would once have approved should now be so threatening to the Association. This was at least in part due to the changed face of technical teaching and the need to protect lecturers in 'non-preferred' subject areas. But there was also every indication that government policy was determined less by the long-term needs of the economy for more skills than by its ideological opposition to the public sector. It certainly had very little to do with the principles of social justice which in the mid-seventies the Education Secretary had hoped the Association could now concentrate upon.

EDUCATION AND UNEMPLOYMENT

Whilst relatively untouched by the student numbers game and more obviously and directly vocational in nature, further education experienced an equally traumatic time during this period. Its bleakest years in terms of enrolments would seem to have been between 1975 and 1980 when all modes other than full-time and sandwich showed a marked decline. From 1980/1, however, enrolments began to pick up again. Indeed, in 1981/2, the number of full-time and sandwich students aged 16-18 studying on non-advanced courses increased by 31,000 or 12 per cent. In addition non-advanced students aged 21 or over increasingly turned to part-time day courses in the colleges, their numbers rising from 149,000 in 1980/1 to 167,000 in 1981/2 in England alone. The total number of students following part-time day courses reached the figure of 272,000 by 1984.[11] Whilst this would indicate a significant increase in the volume of work undertaken by the colleges, overall student numbers in further education establishments increased only marginally in the decade following 1975. As can be seen from Table 6.2, this was due to a marked downturn in the figures for day-release students and also a decline, though somewhat smaller, in the number of evening-only students.

Table 6.2: Enrolments on non-advanced courses at FE establishments in England, 1970-1984 (nos. in thousands)

	1970	1975	1980	1982	1983	1984
Full-time and sandwich	177	256	296	355	344	337
Part-time day release	537	439	419	313	352	368
Other part-time day	113	192	166	241	247	272
Evening only	676	740	573	596	635	642
Total	1503	1627	1454	1505	1578	1619

Source: DES Statistical Bulletin 11/85

The changing fortunes of further education during this period can be explained with reference to two basic facts: mass unemployment on the one hand and the increasing intervention of the Manpower Services Commission (MSC) in providing training schemes for unemployed youth on the other. The increasing numbers of young unemployed contributed to the growth in full-time and sandwich recruitment amongst 16-18 year-olds who might otherwise have found work and to the part-time day courses which the more mature unemployed could also follow for as long as it did not interfere with their availability for work. On the other hand, the continuing decline in Britain's industrial base and the sharp decrease in the number of apprenticeships available were responsible for a massive downturn in the very day-release courses which the ATTI and the TUC had long sought to make universal. This downward trend was reversed only by young people on the various MSC Youth Training Schemes (YTS) whose numbers grew from 32,000 in 1982 to 104,000 in 1983 to 114,000 in 1984.

The MSC was originally set up in 1974 by the Heath administration and started life under the new Labour government. It was to be responsible for manpower planning, industrial training and policies to deal with the already increasing numbers of unemployed. In the spirit of the age, it was a tripartite body based on the Industrial Training Boards which in their turn had equal numbers of employer and trade union representatives. Further education was represented by two local authority members and one from education. A major concern, expressed in the reports of its executive arm, the Training Services Agency, was with 'the great untrained', the estimated 60 per cent of young people then entering employment without any form of further education or training and no chance of continuing education. It was intended that the education service take an active part in the formation of training policy through what were known as Educational Consultative Groups. As such, the body was welcomed by the ATTI.

Increasingly, however, the MSC was forced to concentrate on plans to help the young employed whose numbers were beginning to rise dramatically by the mid-seventies. In October 1976, an MSC report, 'Towards a Comprehensive Manpower Policy', identified youth unemployment as a major area of concern and a working party was set up to study whether or not it was feasible for all young people aged 16-18 who had no job or who were not continuing their studies to have the opportunity of training, of participating in a job creation programme, or of work experience. The result was the Holland Report, published in May 1977, which recommended a unified programme of vocational preparation for unemployment young people based upon both work experience and vocational training. The further education service was to make its contribution to this vocational training and the government announced that it was prepared to make available resources for a further 10,000 full-time equivalent places for 16-18 year-olds over the following three years. Later that same year, an MSC consultative document, 'The Next Steps', outlined the details of the Youth Opportunities Programme (YOPS) and the first of the youth training schemes to deal with mass youth unemployment was born.

The following years of Tory administration saw further cuts in resources for further education at the same time as a massive increase in the funds available to the MSC. In 1980, the Secretary of State for Employment announced that the government was trying to work towards every unemployed 16-17 year-old being guaranteed vocational preparation up to the age of 18. It was hoped that the MSC programmes would cater for 1 in 3 school leavers in 1981 and 1 in 2 in 1982. But despite some obviously very good schemes, YOPs was generally felt to be a failure. Perhaps the most controversy surrounded the Work Experience on Employers Premises schemes (WEEP) which made up about 65 per cent of the programme. Under WEEP, a trainee would work for an employer for six months and receive a training allowance of £25 per week. But the fact that the employer could claim back the £25 led to the very real possibility of job substitution. Furthermore a trainee under such a scheme was entitled to some off-the-job training, whether in a further education college or one of the MSC Skillcentres. It was estimated that some 50 per cent of such trainees did not receive their entitlement. Under such circumstances, it was hardly surprising that many young people simply voted with their feet, especially where there was no possibility of a job on completing the course.[11]

In the face of these problems the government's first major initiative in the field of industrial training was to dismantle 17 of the 24 statutory Industrial Training Boards (much against the MSC's advice) thus abolishing the compulsory levy paid by employers and re-establishing the very 'voluntarism' in the system which had previously been

A Future Secured?

judged so inadequate by both Labour and Tory governments alike. At the same time, in its White Paper, A New Training Initiative: A Programme for Action (December 1982), the government announced an intention to introduce an element of compulsion into a revised Youth Training Scheme (YTS) by confining the scheme to the unemployed and withdrawing Supplementary Benefit from those refusing to take part. A cut in the training allowance from the YOP level of £23.50 to £15 was also proposed. However, such was the outcry against these proposals that an MSC Youth Task Group was set up to develop an alternative approach. Its subsequent report recommended an allowance at the YOP rate, no withdrawal of Supplementary Benefit and a one-year scheme to cover all 16 year-olds not in full-time education. The Secretary of State for Employment, Norman Tebbit, conceded all points and a scheme of 460,000 places was to be implemented by September 1983, on an overall budget of £1 billion. The new schemes were in the majority to be employer-based with some 13 weeks off-the-job training which might or might not take place in the further education sector. Nevertheless, the potential for further education was enormous. The NATFHE Journal, for example, estimated that it could eventually mean some 40,000-80,000 full-time equivalent students for further education, an average of 100 full-time equivalent students per college. At a time when traditional craft-level courses were declining rapidly and a demographic downturn expected, such potential numbers could not be ignored.

But there were dangers as well. For example, there were some within further education who were suspicious of the rise of the MSC from the beginning and these suspicions went much deeper than the fear that the government of the day might be more interested in masking a politically sensitive level of youth unemployment than in rectifying what was generally acknowledged to be an appallingly low level of industrial training in Britain. Rather, they saw in the MSC a potential government tool for changing the whole structure and function of further education in line with what were arguably short-term political expediencies rather than the long-term needs of the economy. For example, David Blunkett, leader of Sheffield City Council, the town in which the MSC had its headquarters, wrote as early as 1975 that:

While the Department of Education and Science

and LEAs throughout the country struggle to find the money to provide FE courses for many different students, a siren song can be heard which offers the money the service so desperately needs. In this instance the money is from the public purse, but a different public purse with different criteria and a different goal - the Department of Employment are offering to pay for the provision of Training Opportunities (TOPs) courses in a variety of subjects. Many colleges feel they are faced with Hobson's choice ...

... Principles established over many years are now to be discarded to meet the immediate need as they see it. Non-compliance with the wishes of those paying the bill will result in such courses going elsewhere. Co-ordination, co-operation and joint objectives have gone out of the window so that while the DES struggle in the face of financial crisis, the TSA has its budget increased, and seemingly takes over where the education service reluctantly leaves off.[13]

The implication here is that competition for scarce resources might induce the local education authorities and the colleges to accept schemes they would otherwise reject. This was especially the case when there were government Skillcentres and private training agencies ready and waiting to do the work for them. Under such circumstances, NATFHE gave the YTS qualified support and concentrated its attentions at local level on gaining representation on the Area Manpower Boards which were responsible for local delivery. Here NATFHE's immediate aims were to ensure quality and limit privatisation. At national level, conference decisions highlighted the increasingly unacceptable level of youth unemployment, the dangers of job substitution and de-skilling and the continued exploitation of many of the young people on the schemes. At the same time the NATFHE Journal carried articles on 'best practice' as illustrated by schemes up and down the country which were working well.

However, with the publication of the government's White Paper, Training for Jobs (January 1984), the tenor of the debate began to shift from one of ambivalence to open hostility both to the YTS and the MSC itself. The White Paper, developed in great secrecy and published without consultation, proposed that 25 per cent of the funds which would normally find their way into further education via the Rate Support Grant should in 1985 go instead to the MSC. This, the White Paper argued, would enable the Commission to 'purchase' more work-related, non-advanced further education and ensure that public sector provision for training and vocational education was more responsive to employment needs. NATFHE described the proposals as 'the most serious threat to face further education in the last forty years' and challenged the government to substantiate its claims that the further education service was unresponsive to employers' needs. Where they had been unresponsive, they admitted, was in their temerity to criticise the inadequacies of YTS and to suggest that it was the government who were not taking vocational education and training seriously.[14] At conference, fears were expressed that 'the next step after central control was privatisation'.[15] There was no guarantee that the 25 per cent of present resources would all come back to the colleges no matter how 'relevant' further education tried to be. Private training agencies would offer narrower courses of dubious quality much more cheaply than the colleges, not least because their staff were paid less and their conditions of service allowed courses to be run on an 'open-all-hours' basis. 'Unless we abolish private YTS,' one delegate argued, 'it will abolish us.'[16] Already by 1985 the Association was reporting that it had gathered 'a mass of evidence showing conclusively that many changes have occurred without consent, have been imposed either by arbitrary decision by local authorities or by the threat of starvation of resources by the government and the MSC'.[17] The potential loss of autonomy and control consequent upon the implementation of Training for Jobs would have been enormous.

However, such was the strength of opposition from both Labour and Tory councils as well as from NATFHE and the TUC that in July of that year the Commission felt unable to implement the proposals, only to be faced by a later directive from the Secretary of State for Employment, Tom King, that they had got to proceed. Then, after a year of what NATFHE described as one of the most prolonged, intense and bitter conflicts in the world of education since 1944 and the departure of David Young from the MSC to the Cabinet, the local education authorities and the MSC agreed to set up a Review Group to work out a compromise. This reported in May 1985 and proposed that Development Plans be prepared by local education authorities in respect of work-related, non-advanced further education after consultation with the MSC, local employers, trade unions and other interested parties. As well as meeting nationally agreed priorities, a good deal of emphasis was to be put on meeting the needs of the local labour market in keeping with the White Paper's definition of 'relevance' and what the Association believed to be its narrowly vocational concept of training which was to be 'firmly work-oriented and lead to jobs'. In this way, local authorities (and by implication the colleges) would have to negotiate with the MSC for resources which had hitherto automatically come their way. In the meantime, the White Paper, <u>Education and Training for Young People</u> (April 1984), announced the extension of the YTS to a two-year scheme and the establishment of the Review of Vocational Qualifications (RVQ) to examine the structure of vocational qualifications within the context of mounting criticism on the part of the government and some employers of the further education system's ability to meet employers' needs.

For their part, NATFHE pointed to the record of both employers and government in failing to provide funds for vocational education and training and to the inadequacies of candyfloss schemes designed to meet the short-term needs of employers rather than effect the regeneration of British industry through the provision of real training for real jobs. In this context, opposition to the YTS reached its height at conference the following year. 'YTS is rotten to the core: it's a national disgrace and it should go,'[18] said one delegate to applause. In the meantime, however, those concerned about the lack of an immediate alternative looked to negotiations on the Development Plans to salvage what they could of the Association's ultimate goal, however much it had been set back, of an integrated system of education and training not only for the 16-19 age-group but for all adults throughout life. This, they argued, could only be achieved within a new tertiary system of post-school education under common regulations.[19] The MSC, with its separate funding and narrow vocationalism had undermined the very basis of this strategy - the unity of both education and training already taking place in the colleges of further education.

DO MORE FOR LESS
At least one of the reasons for the Association's pragmatic response to the dangers of the MSC and the inadequacies of the YTS was that they provided Association members with

A Future Secured?

jobs at a time when the public sector in general was under threat and the further education service was being squeezed. This climate of insecurity together with the obvious need to do something about the tragic problem of youth unemployment made the sort of principled opposition which had been mounted over the negative effects of the cuts somewhat difficult. Indeed, the membership's willingness to embrace the MSC at local level was becoming a source of increasing difficulty for the Association. One of the justifications for locating MSC work outside of the colleges had been the 'inflexibility' inherent in local conditions of service agreements, the basis for which had been negotiated with the Council of Local Authority Associations in 1975 and meant to apply in full from September 1977. This national agreement, the first to cover lecturers in the public sector specified what were to be the maximum class contact hours each grade of lecturer could be asked to do; a maximum week of 30 hours and a maximum year of 36/38 weeks; a maximum continuous teaching session and a minimum summer holiday of six weeks. In addition, remission of class contact hours was to be negotiated locally from a list of eligible duties and overtime payment made for all class contact above the maximum. The agreement was considered to be a real victory for the ATTI and for collective bargaining.

The MSC, on the other hand, organised its courses for up to twelve hours a day, six days a week over 47 weeks of the year. In themselves, however, the conditions of service agreements need not have been a major obstacle to the mounting of MSC courses in the colleges. In fact, the Association had long been involved in 'Extended College Year' agreements which had circumvented some of the difficulties. These, together with casual contracts, might have sufficed where the amount of MSC-funded work was small. Now that it was to become a significant part of the work of the colleges the only solution, as NATFHE saw it, was to employ adequate levels of permanent staff under conditions no less favourable than those already pertaining. When the MSC was already employing 'supervisors' on inferior terms and conditions of service, and when in some colleges conditions had already been seriously eroded, neither the government nor the local authorities were likely to agree.

It was against this background that the Audit Commission published its report Obtaining Better Value

184

from <u>Further Education</u> in June 1985. This report, which was given much publicity in the media, concluded that 'value improvement opportunities' of, on average, £300,000 per college could be made on certain 'performance indicators' such as staff-student ratios and class contact hours. It was made clear that lecturers' terms and conditions of service were considered the key to 'better value for money' in the public sector: 'The reduction in class contact as seniority increases, the lack of minimum class contact hours, teaching years of 33 weeks or less, timetabling arrangements which permit lecturers to claim overtime payments even though they have not met their contractual hours for the year as a whole, are all aspects of the present arrangements requiring attention,' the commissioners argued.[20] Despite what the Association considered to be a detailed refutation of most of the charges and research evidence which estimated a lecturer's weekly load at around 40 hours,[21] the following year's salary negotiations were made conditional upon talks about changes in conditions of service. When those conditions of service had originally been negotiated certain sections of the press had described them as 'a skivers charter' and they were never popular with the local authorities as the employers.[22] Even before the 1986 salary negotiations, certain local authorities had tried unilaterally to increase the maximum class contact hours a lecturer might be expected to work but the opposition they met with at local level in the main thwarted such attempts. By 1986 the employers obviously judged the political climate right to try and impose one huge productivity deal on the college lecturers.

Indeed, there was a good deal of irony surrounding the history of salary negotiations over the ten years leading up to this point. As we have seen, the early sixties saw the increasing intervention of the Minister of State in salary negotiations, not only in terms of the size of the global sum but also in terms of its distribution. The 1965 Remuneration of Teachers Act formalised this position and gave central government a decisive role in the teachers' negotiations with their employers by placing two of its representatives on the management panel of the Burnham Committees. Whilst other teachers' associations were at first ambivalent about this representation, the ATTI opposed it from the start arguing that it interfered with their right to free collective bargaining with their employers.[23] The Association wanted to see instead some form of National

Joint Negotiating Committee which would enable them to negotiate both salaries and conditions of service with their employers without direct government intervention and they took every opportunity they could to call for the repeal of the Act. Their opposition reached its height in the late seventies when after endorsing the policies of the TUC in support of government incomes policies, they found themselves yet again disadvantaged, not only in relation to the private sector but also in relation to other public sector workers. Indeed, the Houghton Relativities Working Party set up by the Burnham Committees in 1978 in part fulfilment of the management panel's 'wholehearted commitment to the principles enunciated in the Houghton Report' reported that an average increase of 24.5 per cent additional to the 1978 settlement would be necessary to restore lecturers' salaries to the levels deemed appropriate by the Houghton Committee five years previously.[24]

In this light, NATFHE put in a 28 per cent salary claim for 1979 and prepared the way for strike action in the face of a 9 per cent offer from the employers and a refusal to consider the various structural reforms proposed by the Association. Arbitration was another possibility. Subsequently, however, enough progress was made on structure for the Association to continue negotiations only to be told by the Secretary of State, Mrs Shirley Williams, that the offer from the employers was too generous to permit. Neither was the government prepared to approve the terms of reference provisionally agreed for the Standing Commission on Pay Comparability (the Clegg Commission), the findings of which were to be payable in two instalments the following year. This intervention at a crucial stage in negotiations brought forth the following outburst from the president of the Association at Conference that year:

> All other comparable groups of local authority workers negotiate pay and conditions of service in a Joint National Council, a JNC, employees on one side, employers - the local authorities - on the other. In Burnham, there are two panels, Teachers and Management, but the actual difference is that on the Management panel sit two Civil Servants, representatives of the Secretary of State. These two Civil Servants can exercise an absolute veto within the Management Panel on any matter that affects the global sum. These two individuals,

representing the Secretary of State, have absolute power to outvote all the representatives of over one hundred local education authorities and prevent them from improving their offer beyond that which the Government has determined. Connoisseurs of Burnham on the Teachers Panel know full well that when the leader of the Management Panel is making an offer you pay no attention to him, you look down the table at the senior of those two very able Civil Servants. Is he looking happy... is he looking grim? Does that mean he's going to use his veto or that this is an unauthorised offer not yet 'cleared' from on high?... From this platform I call upon the Secretary of State to repeal the Remuneration of Teachers' Act... By the repeal of the Act and with the creation of a JNC covering both pay and conditions the Secretary of State could make the greatest contribution to industrial relations in the teaching profession for decades.[25]

Before the matter could be resolved there was a change of government subsequent to which a 9 per cent salary increase was agreed with the employers together with the previously proposed reference to the Standing Commission on Pay Comparability. The Association was not entirely happy with this, preferring instead that negotiations should proceed with their employers on the basis of the findings of the Houghton Relativities Committee. They were especially concerned that the salary increases which the Commission was to recommend would be dependent upon a job evaluation exercise and in their evidence to Clegg they were careful to point out that the lecturers' 'total remuneration package' (working hours, holidays, security of tenure, pensions, stability and fringe benefits) was nothing like as advantageous as it might seem. It did seem at first that they had good cause to worry for early in the new year there were rumours that Clegg might offer little or no increase on this very basis. In the event, however, the Clegg Commission failed in its attempts at job evaluation and the various increases awarded to the lecturers between 1979 and 1980 finally meant that by September 1980 most had received an increase of almost 50 per cent on the salaries which were being paid in March 1979 and Lecturers 1 at the top of the scale an increase of 51 per cent. Whilst these increases were still some 15-20 per cent short of the Houghton levels, they were a source of some considerable satisfaction at a time when the political climate was becoming increasingly unfavourable to the public sector.

Not surprisingly, therefore, thereafter teachers' salaries again began the inevitable decline which resulted finally in 1985 in a massive and prolonged campaign of industrial action on the part of the school teachers in response to a 4 per cent offer in the Burnham Main Committee. The campaign was mounted on the basis of the slogan 'Back to Houghton' and this, too, became the aim of NATFHE who in 1985 were claiming that they needed an increase of 28 per cent to restore Houghton earning power, an increase of 38 per cent to put them in the same position in the general earnings league and an increase of some 43 per cent to keep in line with the average salaries of professional workers.[26] The Association put in a claim of 20.5 per cent as a first step on the road back to Houghton and were offered 4 per cent as the school teachers had been. As a result of a ballot on the offer, some 54 per cent of the votes cast were for strike action which subsequently took place on a selective basis for the first time since the period leading up to Clegg. In July, the management panel increased its offer to some 5 per cent with a further 2 per cent available as from December but conditional upon joint talks on conditions of service to be brought to completion for implementation by September 1986. The Executive recommended acceptance as the best offer that could be obtained in further education under the circumstances (and there was a significant sweetener to the pill in the management panel's acceptance of automatic progression from Lecturer 1 to Lecturer 2, a treasured goal of the Association for the twelve years previous). At about the same time, the local authorities told the government that they wanted an end to the arrangements whereby the government could exercise a veto over the size of pay settlements. They wanted instead to negotiate directly with their own staffs.

At Conference in May that year, those active in the Association had given a clear instruction to their negotiators that there should be no 'trade-off' on salaries and conditions of service. Fears were expressed that the local authorities who had always considered the conditions of service contained in the Association's 'Silver Book' too expensive, would take the opportunity to offer the lecturers a self-financing pay award which would be too attractive to turn down. Others even opposed the very idea of joint negotiations on pay and conditions, long a cornerstone of NATFHE policy, in the context of the current political and economic climate. But the conditional salary offer was accepted, largely on the grounds that perhaps it did not really commit the Association to anything anyway and what limited industrial action there had been was called off.

The following year, the Association accepted a 5.5 per cent salary settlement and reaffirmed its commitment to the sort of structural review agreed the previous year. A long list of matters 'to be negotiated to conclusion' by October 1986 had been set out in the National Joint Negotiating Committee (set up in 1980 to negotiate conditions of service with the employers and, it was hoped, eventually salaries as well) which from the management side included the reform of the grading of courses system and an examination of the system of class contact hours whereby the more senior and experienced a lecturer, the less teaching they were expected to do, long matters of concern to NATFHE as well. More ominously, however, and especially in view of the school teachers dispute, there were proposals for 'staff development' and appraisal on the agenda. In the light of the Audit Commission's Report and the original agreement to look at conditions of service in the interests of 'economy and efficiency', many active within the Association viewed the employers' interest in class contact hours with considerable apprehension. Indeed, at Conference in 1986, the General Secretary renewed the Association's call for the repeal of the Remuneration of Teachers Act in terms designed to quell the fears within the Association that their conditions of service were under threat:

> We are not in the business of selling our conditions of service which are the basis of the defence of our members jobs. We are in the business of negotiating improved conditions of service which will form the basis of a healthy and expanding FHE service for the decades beyond... Okay, maybe management will have some things to say we won't like. Okay, there will have to be disputes; there will have to be bargaining and maybe compromises on both sides as the years go by. But none of the objectives ... I have mentioned are possible if

> mature trade unionists and their employers aren't
> sitting down talking about a total package of the
> work we do and what we're paid for.[27]

In fact, optimism grew that an agreement might be reached
with the employers which would provide the basis of a joint
approach to the government for more resources, just like
the ill-fated 'Coventry Agreement' struck between the
school teachers and the local authorities in May of that
year.

The talks which took place in Nottingham in October
provided no such opportunity, however, as the employers
refused to discuss any package until agreement was reached
on their proposals for a standard 22 hours of weekly class
contact for all lecturers, with the option of increasing these
to 26 hours for specified periods of up to ten weeks. The
talks broke down and NATFHE initiated a ban on overtime
and voluntary duties from the beginning of the new year in
an attempt to get the employers back to the negotiating
table in a more resaonable frame of mind. At the request of
NATFHE, the employers did come back to the negotiating
table six months later in March 1987, but there was little
change in their frame of mind. There was an increase in
money available - NATFHE calculated it as an average
increase of 7.1 per cent, with more going to the higher
grades - but there was at first little change in the
employers' attitudes to class contact hours or averaging.
Proposals to increase the length of the working year and
working week also remained, as did an attempt at definition
of the lecturer's role to include duties for which remission
of class contact hours had usually been available. The
Executive Committee considered the proposals totally
unacceptable and prepared to ballot the membership on a
programme of escalating industrial action, including strike
action. Subsequently, the employers modified their position
on class contact hours but in such a way as to distinguish
between lecturers in further and in higher education. All
talks at this stage were 'without prejudice', which meant
that neither side was committing itself to anything, possibly
because of the imminent General Election and the
significance the outcome might have for the whole of the
public sector.

A PROFESSION DIVIDED
The breakdown of talks in the newly constituted NJC was

unfortunate in more ways than one. February of that year had seen the long awaited repeal of the Remuneration of Teachers Act but in circumstances far from designed to improve industrial relations, at least as far as the school teachers were concerned. After a sustained campaign of industrial action, the school teachers had at last reached an agreement with their employers, the proposed settlement from which was turned down by the Secretary of State for Education, Kenneth Baker, in favour of his own. Claiming teacher disunity as the reason for their inability to reach a settlement, he proposed legislation to abolish the Burnham Committees in favour, for the time being at least, of an 'Advisory Body' which would 'consult' but not negotiate with the teachers' unions on pay and conditions. It would report to the Secretary of State who would publish salaries and conditions by statutory instrument. The Secretary of State might or might not take the advice of this 'Advisory Body'. Curiously NATFHE was not included in these proposals and was left instead to negotiate both salaries and conditions of service with the employers in a manner which they both saw fit. So at the same time as the teachers in the schools (albeit 'temporarily') lost their rights to collective bargaining, the lecturers in the colleges of further and higher education, it seemed, gained theirs in a forum long demanded by the Association.

Despite the fact that the Secretary of State justified the abolition of Burnham in terms of the teachers' associations inability to agree amongst themselves, the sequence of events would indicate that it was their inability to agree the settlement which he preferred which led to the impasse. Ironically, Burnham had been born out of the struggles of the school teachers for better pay, now it was to be abolished because of them. There is no doubt that the lecturers in the colleges were both unable and unwilling to mount the sort of sustained campaign over pay which their colleagues in the schools had done. They were unwilling at least in part because, for the most part, they were better off than their colleagues in the schools and in a climate of job loss, both inside further and higher education and in the economy as a whole, they felt themselves relatively privileged. They were unable not only because of their felt lack of industrial muscle, but also because of the difficulties of uniting a membership around tactics which would have a common effect and a common cause. We have seen already how the structure of the profession has tended to divide the lecturers the one against the other - technologists vs teachers of humanities and the social sciences, teachers in higher vs teachers in further education, teachers on higher grades vs lower grades and so on. During the years of expansion the technologists held their jobs at the expense of the social scientists who might grudgingly struggle with high staff-student ratios necessary to disguise the technologists' underemployment. With NAB and the government's preferred and non-preferred subject areas, it was the turn of the social scientist and the teacher of humanities to feel under threat, whilst accountants, lawyers and those conversant with the new technology were appointed at higher grades and promoted earlier to compete with the higher pay in industry. Even the potentially unifying impact of the cuts thus had an individualising effect as they fell unevenly between sectors and between institutions. Within institutions they were met with premature early retirement schemes (welcome to some) and individual lecturers taking on increased work loads and loss of remission. As one article in the NATFHE Journal put it:

> The system now trades on people's professional commitment to overcome gaps in institutional provision... Many staff find it difficult to confront the process of erosion collectively because it often proceeds by confronting people with individual dilemmas - whether to accept one or two additional students in a seminar group or reorganise options in a degree programme to take account of staff losses. It is a process designed to enhance feelings of powerlessness.[28]

These, then, were the difficulties facing a union whose policy was for a comprehensive system of post-school education uniting teachers in public sector further and higher education and, eventually, across the binary divide. The question of trade unionism vs professionalism had been resolved and the unity of both demonstrated in action over the effects of the education cuts on such matters of principle as standards and student access. This at least was one legacy of the Thatcher government after eight years in office. The limits to trade union action over collective issues became increasingly a question of tactics than of strategy. In a year when the miners had been forced back to work, it had been unlikely in the extreme that the college lecturers would take on the government over salaries, especially when it was difficult to devise sanctions which would harm the employer more than the students and when there was a general belief that the government did not much care about the state education system anyway. Nevertheless, if not over salaries alone, then over conditions of service, college lecturers did show that they were prepared to exercise an overtime ban which did threaten courses and students, in the short term at least.

Against these gains, however, the forces for disunity and fragmentation were gathering pace in the eighties exacerbated, whether deliberately or not, by government policies on funding and provision. In higher education, they reached their most threatening with the government's White Paper, Higher Education, Meeting the Challenge, published in March 1987. In this White Paper, Mr Kenneth Baker proposed that all the English polytechnics and all other major colleges with more than 55 per cent advanced-level work (some 82 institutions in all) should be removed from local authority control and come under central government control via a Polytechnics and Colleges Funding Council appointed by the Secretary of State from industry and commerce and from higher education itself. The institutions would have corporate status under these arrangements and in line with government policy that education should be more 'relevant', local and regional industry and commerce together with the professions would have strong representation on their governing bodies. In addition, the term 'public sector higher education' was to be replaced with reference instead to 'the polytechnics and colleges sector', more appropriate in view of the government's attempts to encourage private, rather than public funding. In similar vein, 'grants' and 'allocations' were to be replaced by 'contracts', either with the private sector or with the funding council again as an encouragement to seek private funds but also denoting the colleges' lack of entitlement to public funds unless specific educational objectives, most notably responsiveness to employers' needs, were met.[29] Under corporate status, the governing bodies of the individual institutions would become the employers of the college staffs.

The proposals generated a great deal of hostility from both the local authorities and from NAB, whose own 'Good Management Practice' report recommending corporate status but with local authority links was about to be published. Indeed, such was the ill-feeling on the part of the NAB committee at its summary dismissal (the government planned to disband it in 1988, even though the new funding council would not be in place until the following year), that it refused to sanction a programme of work by the NAB secretariat which would lead to its winding up. In fact the only body to support the proposals wholeheartedly was the Association of Polytechnic teachers (APT), NATFHE's arch-rival in the polytechnic sector, with the Committee of Directors of Polytechnics bringing up the rear. And herein lay the great danger for NATFHE. Not only would further and higher education be split off from one another through the severance of the local authority link, but the lecturers in each sector would cease to have a common employer. This had long been the aim of the APT which believed that the parity of prestige with the universities which had been promised with the original binary policy could only be achieved through central control and funding. More importantly, they believed that their lack of parity with the university teachers both in terms of salary and conditions of service was a product of NATFHE's concern to get a better deal for further education at the expense of polytechnic lecturers. Whilst NATFHE recruited some 55 per cent of polytechnic lecturers (as opposed to some 80 per cent of lecturers in other major institutions), the APT remained relatively small, their position not helped by the fact that the local authorities refused to recognise them. Early in the eighties, however, the government gave them a place on the teachers' panel in the Burnham Further Education Committee and via an amendment to Baker's Education Bill in the Lords, they found their way onto the newly constituted National Joint Negotiating Committee. Their recruiting material stressed the sectional interests of polytechnic lecturers, NATFHE's, the unity of interest between lecturers in further and higher education, not least because of their common employers. With the possibility of central funding and an attempt by the local authorities to impose conditions of service many in higher education might feel more appropriate to further education, the very basis of this rationale could be undermined and NATFHE might be in a considerably weaker position.

But even if under these circumstances, the majority of polytechnic lecturers remained loyal to their union, the proposals incorporated in the 1987 White Paper would still present NATFHE with difficult industrial relations problems, not least from the possibility of a multiplicity of employers and local variations to national agreements which might very well not be above the minima agreed nationally, if indeed any national negotiations were intended to take place given the government's well-publicised preference for local negotiations as a more accurate reflection of market forces. Add to this the possibility of increased competition between institutions for 'contracts', the interest of the MSC in making inroads into higher education and the dangers of privatisation and fragmentation were very real indeed. That morale in the colleges had already been damaged could be seen from an eve of election poll conducted by The Times Higher Education Supplement where some 65 per cent of the lecturers in the polytechnics and colleges of higher education had seriously considered leaving their present post, a figure very different from that pertaining in the seventies. The reasons given for this disillusionment were low academic salaries, a climate of low morale in higher education consequent upon government policies, increased teaching and administrative loads consequent upon the cuts and the related question of too little time for research.[30] Indeed, so serious was the threat considered to be in the spring of 1987, that many within the Association were arguing that the future integrity not only of public sector further and higher education but of NATFHE itself depended very much on the outcome of the imminent General Election. Should the Thatcher government be returned for a third term of office, the association of teachers which had grown and matured into a professional trade union with the growth and maturity of their sector of education might find it a very difficult task indeed to defend not only its members interests but the very basis of its existence.

NOTES

1. NATFHE Journal, March 1977.
2. John Bevan, Deputy Education Officer, ILEA cited in the NATFHE Journal, May 1979. Mr Bevan, himself a past president of NATFHE, was later to become secretary to the National Advisory Body for Higher Education (NAB).
3. Cited in the NATFHE Journal, October 1979.
4. 'What the Government is Doing to Advanced Further Education', NATFHE Journal, June/July 1980. For a detailed analysis of the technical shortcomings of this initial capping of the pool see Peter Knight, 'The Advanced Further

Education Pool', <u>NATFHE Journal</u>, October 1980.

5. General Secretary's Address, <u>NATFHE Journal</u>, June/July 1980.

6. Ibid.

7. Speaking on The World Tonight, Radio 4, 20 March 1980. Cited in 'What the Government is Doing to Advanced Further Education', ibid. June/July 1980.

8. 'Comment', <u>NATFHE Journal</u>, March 1980.

9. See, for example, 'Countdown to the Green Paper', ibid. October 1984. During this period both the NAB and NATFHE reluctantly acquiesced in this increase in numbers in the name of protecting access. By 1986, however, the process of erosion had gone so far that even the National Advisory Body called a halt and refused to accept the government's target figures on student numbers, this time in the name of protecting the unit of resource. See 'Dicing with HE', <u>NATFHE Journal Supplement</u>, March 1986 for a discription of the political manoeuvring on the part of both NAB and the government at this stage.

10. For a useful summary of the major points of concern in the Green Paper see Nan Whitbread and Alan Taylor-Russell, <u>Higher Education and the Nation's Future, Replies to the Green Paper</u> (Council for Educational Advance, 1986).

11. NATFHE Memorandum, <u>FHE Structure</u>, 1985, pp. 2-19.

12. For further details and worries about the operation of the YTS see 'Quality in YOP', <u>NATFHE Journal</u>, May 1981 and 'The Youth Training Scheme, Hopes and Fears', ibid. May 1983.

13. Quoted in David Blunkett, 'Has the Education Service Left It Too Late?', ibid. November 1982.

14. 'News', ibid. March 1984.

15. Conference Report, ibid. July/August 1984.

16. Ibid.

17. <u>FHE Structure</u>, p.7.

18. Conference Report, NATFHE Journal, June/July 1986.

19. See <u>Planning for Change in FE - An Alternative Strategy</u>, NATFHE discussion document, 1986 for a full statement of the tertiary ideal.

20. Quoted in 'Do More for Less', <u>NATFHE Journal</u>, October 1985.

21. See, for example, Bob Kelney & David Parkes, <u>Responsibility and Responsiveness</u> (Association of Metropolitan Authorities/Further Education Staff College,

1985) which challenged the government's criticism of FE's 'inflexibility' and unwillingness to meet employer demand through eight case studies of college responses to the changing demands of the previous five years.

22. It is worth quoting the remarks of Jack Hendy, president of the Association in 1976/7 during the period when the Conditions of Service Agreement was being implemented.

> During the past year I had occasion to participate in a rather bitter controversy with a newspaper (now said to be in economic difficulty) which had described our Conditions of Service Agreement as 'A skiver's charter'... I make no apologies to anyone for our real achievements in this sphere... There are still a few recalcitrant authorities which have not yet implemented those conditions which it is agreed shall be the national minimum, and such authorities are at present being rightly subjected to all the persuasive processes which are available to us either by trade union law or trade union practice.

NATFHE Journal, August/September 1977.

23. See R.D.Coates, 'The Teachers' Associations and the Restructuring of Burnham', British Journal of Educational Studies, June 1972, pp.192-294 for a detailed analysis of the teachers' response to the Remuneration of Teachers Act.

24. See 'The Background to Clegg', NATFHE Journal, December 1979 and 'Evidence to Clegg', November 1979.

25. President's Address, ibid. June/July 1979.

26. General Secretary's Address, ibid. June/July 1985.

27. Ibid. June/July 1986.

28. 'Poor Relation Status: The Enemy of Quality', ibid. November 1985.

29. For a useful summary of the major proposals incorporated in the White Paper see The Times Higher Education Supplement 10 April 1987.

30. Ibid. 5 June 1987. The poll was conducted in 83 polytechnics, universities and colleges of higher education amongst a representative sample of 497 lecturers. Lecturers were also asked about their voting intentions and attitudes to certain aspects of current education policy.

Bibliography

Argles, M. (1964) South Kensington to Robbins, Longmans, London.

Armstrong, Peter, Bob Carter, Chris Smith, Theo Nichols (1986) White Collar Workers, Trade Unions and Class, Croom Helm, London.

Association of Teachers in Technical Institutions (1955) The First Half Century.

Bain, G.S., D.Coates and V.Ellis (1973) Social Stratification and Trade Unionism, Heinemann, London.

Banks, O. Parity and Prestige in English Secondary Education (1955) Routledge and Kegan Paul, London.

Baron, G. (1952) 'The Secondary Schoolmaster, 1895-1914', unpublished PhD thesis, University of London.

_____ (1954), 'The Teachers' Registration Movement', British Journal of Educational Studies, May 1954.

Blackburn, R.M. (1973) Union Character and Social Class, Batsford, London.

_____ and K. Prandy (1965) 'White Collar Unionization: A Conceptual Framework', British Journal of Sociology, XVI, pp. 111-22.

Blalock, H.M. (1959) 'Status Consciousness: A Dimensional Analysis', Social Forces, 37, pp. 243-8.

Blau, Peter and Richard W. Scott (1963) Formal Organizations: A Comparative Approach, Routledge and Kegan Paul, London.

Blum, Albert, A. (1969) Teachers' Unions and Associations: A Comparative Study, University of Illinois Press, Chicago.

Board of Education (1926) Survey of Technical and Further Education in England and Wales.

Bratchell, D.F. (1968) The Aims and Organization of Further Education, Pergamon, Oxford.

Bulmer, M. (ed) (1975) Working Class Images of Society, Routledge and Kegan Paul, London.

Burgess, T. and J. Pratt (1970) Policy and Practice, The Colleges of Advanced Technology, Allen Lane, London.

Burke, V. (1971) Teachers in Turmoil, Penguin, Harmondsworth.

Cantor, L.H. and I.F. Roberts (1972) Further Education in England and Wales, 2nd edn, Routledge and Kegan Paul, London.

Cardwell, D.S.L. (1957) The Organization of Science in England, Heinemann, London.

Carr-Saunders, A.M. and P.A. Wilson (1933) The Professions, Oxford University Press, Oxford.

Carter, Bob (1986) 'Trade Unionism and the New Middle Class' in Peter Armstrong et al., White Collar Workers, Trade Unions and Class.

Charlton, D., W. Gent and B. Scammells (1971) The Administration of Technical Colleges, Manchester University Press, Manchester.

Coates, R.D. (1972a) Teachers' Unions and Interest Group Politics, Cambridge University Press, Cambridge.

_____ (1972b) 'The Teachers' Associations and the Restructuring of Burnham', British Journal of Educational Studies, 20, pp. 192-204.

Cole, S. (1969) The Unionization of Teachers: A Case Study of the UFT, Praeger, New York.

Corwin, R.G. (1970) Militant Professionalism, Appleton-Century-Crofts, New York.

Cotgrove, S.F. (1958) Technical Education and Social Change, Allen and Unwin, London.

Crosland, A. (1967) 'The Structure and Development of Higher Education', speech at Lancaster University in Eric Robinson, The New Polytechnics.

Dent, H.C. (1949) Part-time Education in Great Britain, Turnstile Press, London.

Elliott, P. (1972) The Sociology of the Professions, Macmillan, London.

Etzioni, A. (1969) The Semi-Professions and their Organization, Collier-Macmillan, New York.

Foden, F. (1961) 'A History of Technical Examinations in England to 1918', unpublished PhD thesis, University of Reading.

Friedson, E. (1973) 'Professionalization and the Organization of Middle-class Labour in Post-Industrial Society' in Halmos, The Personal Service Society.

Halmos, P. (1970) The Personal Service Society, Constable, London.

_____ (ed) (1973) 'Professionalization and Social Change', Sociological Review Monograph, No. 20.

Bibliography

Halsey A.H. and Martin Trow (1971) The British Academics, Faber and Faber, London.

Harbinson, F.H. (1954) 'Collective Bargaining and American Capitalism' in A. Kornhauser et al., Industrial Conflict.

Haug, M. (1973) 'Deprofessionalization: An Alternative Hypothesis For the Future' in Halmos, Professionalization and Social Change.

Hyman, R. and I. Brough (1975) Social Values and Industrial Relations, Blackwell, Oxford.

_____ and R. Price (1983) The New Working Class, Macmillan, London.

Johnson, T.J. (1972) Professions and Power, Macmillan, London.

Kelney, Bob and David Parkes (1985) Responsibility and Responsiveness, Association of Metropolitan Authorities/Further Education Staff College.

Kornhauser, A., R. Dubin and A.M. Ross (eds) (1954) Industrial Conflict, McGraw-Hill, New York.

Lewis, R. and A. Maude (1952) Professional People, Phoenix House, London.

Locke, M. (1974) 'Government' in Pratt and Burgess, Polytechnics: A Report, pp. 149-71.

Liebermann, M. (1956) Education as a Profession, Prentice-Hall, Englewood Cliffs N.J.

Lockwood, D. (1958) The Blackcoated Worker, Allen and Unwin, London.

Manzer, R.A. (1970) Teachers and Politics, Manchester University Press, Manchester.

Millis, C.T. (1925) Technical Education, Its Development and Aims, Arnold, London.

Mills, C. Wright (1951) White Collar, Oxford University Press, New York.

National Association of Teachers in Further and Higher Education (1985) Memorandum, FHE Structure.

_____ (1986) Planning for Change in FE - An Alternative Strategy.

Ogza, J. and M. Lawn (1981) Teachers, Professionalism and Class, Falmer, Sussex.

Perkin, H. (1969) Key Profession: History of the Association of University Teachers, Routledge and Kegan Paul, London.

Prandy, K. (1965) Professional Employees, Faber, London.

Pratt, J. and T. Burgess (1974) Polytechnics: A Report, Pitman, London.

Price, R. (1983) 'White-Collar Unions: Growth Character and

Attitudes in the 1970s' in Hyman and Price, The New Working Class.

Roberts, B.C., R. Loveridge and J. Gennard (1972) Reluctant Militants, Heinemann, London.

Robinson, E. (1968) The New Polytechnics, Penguin Education Special, Harmondsworth.

Richardson, W.A. (1939) The Technical College, Its Organization and Administration, Oxford University Press, Oxford.

Routh, G. (1966) 'White Collar Unions in the United Kingdom' in A. Sturmthal (ed) White Collar Trade Unions.

Silverleaf, J. and J. Bradley Making the Grade: Careers in Further Education, National Foundation for Educational Research.

Smith, Chris (1986) 'Engineers, Trade Unionism and TASS' in Peter Armstrong et al., White Collar Workers, Trade Unions and Class.

Strauss, G. (1954) 'White Collar Unions Are Different', Harvard Business Review, XXXII, pp. 73-82.

Sturmthal, A. (ed) (1967) White Collar Trade Unions, University of Illinois Press, Chicago.

Sykes, A.J.H. (1965) 'Some Differences in the Attitudes of Clerical and Manual Workers', Sociological Review, XIII, pp. 297-310.

Tipton, B. (1973) Conflict and Change in a Technical College, Hutchinson, London.

———— (1972) 'Some Organizational Characteristics of a Technical College', Research in Education, no. 7.

Tropp, A. (1957) The School Teachers, Heinemann, London.

———— (1954) 'Factors Affecting the Status of the School Teacher in England and Wales', Transactions of the Second World Congress of Sociology, vol. II, International Sociological Association, pp. 166-74.

Venables, E. (1967) The Young Worker at College, Faber, London.

Venables, P.F.R. (1956) Technical Education, Its Aims, Organization and Future Development, Bell, London.

Webb, Beatrice (1915) 'English Teachers and their Professional Organization' Special Supplement, New Statesman, 25 September and 2 October 1915.

Webb, Sidney (1898) 'The London Polytechnic Institutes', Special Reports on Educational Subjects, Cd. 8943, vol. ii.

———— (1904) London Education, Longmans, London.

Bibliography

Whitbread, Nan and Alan Taylor Russell (1986) <u>Higher Education and the Nation's Future, Replies to the Green Paper</u>, Council for Educational Advance.

Index

Index